HOW
TO
RETREAT

HOW TO RETREAT

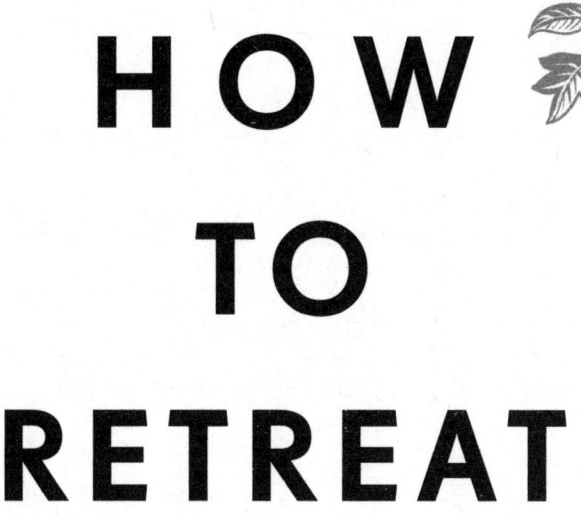

A Guide to Stepping Away from
the Everyday to Find Space
for Your Self

CAROLINE SYLGE

RODALE
NEW YORK

Rodale Books
An imprint of Random House
A division of Penguin Random House LLC
1745 Broadway, New York, NY 10019
rodalebooks.com | randomhousebooks.com
penguinrandomhouse.com

Copyright © 2026 by Hut on a Hill, Ltd.

Penguin Random House values and supports copyright. Copyright fuels creativity, encourages diverse voices, promotes free speech, and creates a vibrant culture. Thank you for buying an authorized edition of this book and for complying with copyright laws by not reproducing, scanning, or distributing any part of it in any form without permission. You are supporting writers and allowing Penguin Random House to continue to publish books for every reader. Please note that no part of this book may be used or reproduced in any manner for the purpose of training artificial intelligence technologies or systems.

Rodale & Plant with colophon is a registered trademark of
Penguin Random House LLC.

Published in the United Kingdom by Rider Books, an imprint of
Ebury Publishing, a division of Penguin Random House UK, London.

ISBN 978-0-593-98118-4
Ebook ISBN 978-0-593-98119-1

Printed in the United States of America

1st Printing

First U.S. Edition

BOOK TEAM: Production editor: Mark Birkey • Managing editor: Allie Fox • Production manager: Angela McNally

The authorized representative in the EU for product safety and compliance is Penguin Random House Ireland, Morrison Chambers, 32 Nassau Street, Dublin D02 YH68, Ireland. https://eu-contact.penguin.ie

*To my friend and fellow retreater Victoria Spicer,
for her trust and unwavering support.*

To my husband Tom, for being both my rock and my rock star.

*To my daughter Annoushka, for making me laugh,
and for opening up my heart.*

CONTENTS

Introduction   1
How to use this book   11
Your Retreat Toolkit   15

PURGE

Retreat for an hour: Clear your mind   47
Retreat for a day: Refresh yourself   51
Retreat for longer: Declutter your stuff   58

CONNECT

Retreat for an hour: Journal   69
Retreat for a day: Garden   74
Retreat for longer: Be kind   82

CREATE

Retreat for an hour: Make a mark   97
Retreat for a day: Find your flow   100
Retreat for longer: Be an artist   108

NURTURE

Retreat for an hour: Embody   119
Retreat for a day: Treat yourself   126
Retreat for longer: Stay put   134

TRUST

Retreat for an hour: Affirm	143
Retreat for a day: Choose gratitude	146
Retreat for longer: Practise self-reliance	152

RECLAIM

Retreat for an hour: De-excite	163
Retreat for a day: Say no	169
Retreat for longer: Unplug	177

SETTLE

Retreat for an hour: Breathe	191
Retreat for a day: Be mindful	199
Retreat for longer: Go into silence	208

PLAN

Retreat for an hour: Design your day	221
Retreat for a day: Trim your choices	226
Retreat for longer: Re-imagine your life	235

References	253
Resources	261
Retreat Poems	271
Acknowledgements	277
Biography	279

INTRODUCTION

*'Tell me, what is it you plan to do with
your one wild and precious life?'*
Mary Oliver, 'The Summer Day'

I first read the compelling words in the epigraph above on a writing retreat in my twenties. I didn't know what I wanted to do with my life at the time, and I hadn't thought of it as being either wild or precious. Oliver's words made me want to make the most of things. To move away from the situations and self-sabotaging thoughts that were dragging me down, and instead take a more sustaining and remarkable path.

Since then, for more than thirty years, 'retreating' in all its forms has helped me do just that. To find different tracks to explore, and to honour my life as something that is wild and precious, as Oliver's remarkable poem puts it. It's why I'd like to share the practice of retreating with you, through this book, and, I hope, inspire you to retreat too.

Where does retreating come from?

For as long as there have been human societies, there have been those who have chosen to retreat from them. The word in English stems from the Old French word *retret*, which comes from the Latin *retrahere*, meaning to 'pull back'. Arguably, the practice began as a spiritual one. For centuries, people from multiple traditions across the globe have physically withdrawn from the world to solitary, silent places in nature on a mission to find meaning in their existence. They may not have had journals or sleep schedules, but they knew the importance of taking time out in remote spots, both with themselves and with their various 'gods'.

As far back as the Vedic period of India over 3,500 years ago, yogis, sages, ascetics and renunciates were retreating to forests, mountains and caves to contemplate. Indigenous peoples across continents were taking solitary journeys into nature, to use vision quests and fasts to find connection. Taoist practitioners headed for the Asian hills to meditate, while Buddhists established monasteries and nunneries as spiritual hubs where monks and nuns devoted years – sometimes lifetimes – to self-study.

Hermits in the Egyptian desert, meanwhile, looked for places to pray apart from society. Nomads elsewhere practised rituals and venerated ancestors as they travelled across spectacular landscapes, living in harmony with the natural world. Christians embraced pilgrimage as a form of spiritual getaway, while their anchorites and anchoresses took 'staying put' to a whole new level, choosing to live in intense enclosure, devoting their lives to poverty and prayer.

By the tenth century, Sufis were using music, sacred poetry and whirling to deepen their experience of spiritual retreating, known to them as *khalwa*. By the seventeenth century, Quakers were gathering together in silence to nurture deep listening and foster friendship in simple, peaceful settings. By the nineteenth century, Catholic laypeople, as well as their clergy, had begun the practice of retreating too.

What is retreating today?

Step forwards into the twenty-first century and many of these enriching practices of withdrawal and connection continue. The ancient impulse to step back, regroup and renew oneself is alive and well everywhere – no faith necessarily required. Contemporary retreats tap into this delightful tapestry of traditions but give them a modern twist. For the guests who attend them, retreating is now less about dogma, and more about creating space for rest, reflection and personal growth.

Whatever your beliefs, or if you have none, retreating is a journey to the centre of your inner life. Withdrawing in order to advance. Slowing down in order to reenergise. Taking yourself away from everyday busyness, and into your being. Helping you to find out who you are in this moment, and how you might want to connect differently with yourself, your tribe, with nature and the world around you. Resetting yourself, so that you can live your life more effectively when you return to it.

Today's retreat can still be a pilgrimage, involve a monastic-style space, a visit to an ashram, extensive silence or Meditation. It can also take the form of a Yoga or hiking holiday, a week at a health spa, a nurturing break led by a therapist, a coaching escape to find a new direction, or even a relaxing weekend in a woodland bolthole.

In this book I'd also like to reclaim retreating as something we can do by ourselves, without having to attend a hosted retreat. As a place, space or practice that allows us to find the rest, replenishment and renewal that we need, in a space of our choosing, wherever we are in our lives. Retreating has always helped humans cope with life's demands, and today it can belong to us all, at a time when the need to 'press pause' away from the stress, digital overload and general overwhelm of daily life has never been greater.

In this way a retreat can also be a quiet moment with yourself in the corner of a busy room. A mindful walk in your local park, or a rejuvenating session on a massage bed during a challenging week. A painting class or a therapy session. Your own home, or other chosen space, for a self-directed hour, day, weekend or week of retreating, with self-care woven into every part of it.

Retreating today is about being and feeling well in yourself, and yet it doesn't have to focus on what we all habitually think of as 'health'. What one person might get from a Qigong session, another person might get from a pottery class. Being 'well' means different things to different people. What does it mean to you?

We all already micro-retreat when we take a break inside our everyday lives. My dad, Herbie, likes 'to sit in the early morning sun and count my blessings'. My mum, Ann, 'to dead head the roses, breathing in their glorious scent'. For my husband Tom, it's a surf or playing guitar. For my daughter, Annoushka, it's listening to music or dancing freely in her room. For friends of all ages it's to hula-hoop on a beach, watch the sun rise over a moor, take a sea dip, stroke the dog or the cat, make art, go on phone-free walks, have a cup of tea in the sunshine, read a novel, play the piano, sing or write a song, climb a scary cliff, cycle or have a game of tennis, play records in a shed, potter in a greenhouse, or daydream.

You don't have to be a particular type of person to retreat. You don't have to be spiritual, a vegan, into Yoga, the owner of a shawl, a 'stretchy' person, or someone with oodles of time on your hands – although, of course, you can be any or all of those things. Retreating is an empowering, life-affirming act for anyone, that honours both yourself and those around you. It takes FOMO, the 'fear of missing out', and turns it into the joy of doing so, whether you're having an early night, gifting yourself a pyjama day, choosing water over wine (or wine over water – see Treat yourself, p. 126), or something else.

Retreating is a personal experience that will mean different things to different people at different times. How you need to retreat, and your personal version of it, will be defined by you, and change as you change, moment by moment, and throughout the stages of your life. I hope this book will meet you wherever you are, and help you start retreating at your own comfort level.

What retreating is not

Retreating is not a 'cure' for human emotion. Life can be supremely provoking, and retreating isn't going to stop you feeling bored, sad, lonely, angry, anxious, jealous or any other agitating feelings. But it might just help you learn strategies to deal with those human emotions better. To work through them, forget them, find the support you need for them, or let them go, all so you can get on with the very important and often interesting job of being human.

Retreats are also not a random collection of wellbeing practices, which can in themselves become unhelpful distractions if we are not fully present when we do them. We can easily go through the motions of a Yoga practice, say, or scribble things mindlessly in our journal, rather than truly listening to what our body or mind is trying to tell us in that moment. Retreating gives meaningful structure and intention to wellbeing activities, so that, hopefully, we are not just following the latest wellness trends on autopilot. It helps us consciously learn basic principles of self-respect and living that will sustain us in our daily lives.

Finally, retreats aren't there to 'perfect' you, or entice you into a perpetual cycle of self-help. They can help us know when to stop and to let things be. To change from within if we need to, to rest and replenish when we want to, to try out new things when we can, but also to embrace our imperfections, so we can be in and of the world, and live well within it.

Why retreat?

'Go some distance away, because the work appears smaller, more of it can be taken in at a glance, and a lack of harmony or proportion is rapidly seen.' This advice comes from one of history's greatest minds, Leonardo da Vinci, who was writing at the height of the Italian Renaissance. He knew that to pull back from a situation gives you a better perspective on it. So what do *you* need to get perspective on?

In the case of retreating, your body and mind, and the life you have temporarily left, are the 'work' da Vinci refers to – *you* are a work of art. By 'going some distance away' from your everyday stresses and strains, retreating equips you to handle yourself, and your life, when you return to them.

Retreating practices today can bring us strength and self-sufficiency, and uncover our authentic voice, away from the crowd, our inner critic and our phones. They can help us work through a situation that's been niggling us and open up our hearts, so we can connect with other people. They can unleash our creativity and help us feel truly well.

You might want to retreat for peace and deep rest. For sanctuary and clarity. To move in nature, then sit somewhere pretty for a long while. To change the direction of your career or relationship. To work through grief, anxiety or loneliness. To experience new things and escape daily chores. To calm yourself down, or give yourself a kickstart.

Future generations may look back at us and marvel that we were online so much of the time, or that we seemed to revel in our constant busyness. Who knows? Meanwhile, we are alive in the here and now, and living longer than humans ever have, so we may as well make the best of it. I believe retreating helps us do just that.

Are you ready to retreat?

No one can retreat for you, or push you into it. It's not like school homework or something delegated to you by your boss. You need to want to retreat to do so effectively. So, before deciding how you need to retreat, ask yourself – are you ready?

You'll know you're ready to retreat when you get that feeling you want the world to stop. When you're craving quiet, or feeling overwhelmed. Perhaps you need help making a decision about something that's important to you? Or to get away from your various electronic devices for more than just an hour. You might want the space and time to do something creative. To move your body more, in ways that feel good. To have a therapist dig into the remarkable tension you are holding in your back or shoulders. To go into a forest just to breathe. To stop trying so hard with everyone and everything. Any or all of the above, and more.

Be aware that while retreating can be joyful and relaxing, betterment and personal growth can also take work. Your preferred way to retreat may not be living alone in a forest for twenty years, or walking barefoot across scorching ground for days, as spiritual seekers might have done in eras past to find their true path. But looking after yourself, and sowing the seeds of change, takes preparation and dedication, and can be challenging. Just know that retreating can often lead you to the very freedoms that you seek. When you are ready, go ahead and make a commitment to yourself (see Retreat Toolkit, p. 15).

What is this book, and why listen to me?

This book is intended as an antidote to contemporary life. A path of suggestions to follow, to help you look after both your mental and physical health. It aims to reclaim retreating as something that everyone can do, and to enable you to personalise what it means to you. It's a celebration of the idea that 'retreat' doesn't have to mean one thing, and that it can shift as you do.

There's a reason this guide to retreating is a physical book and not an online guide. Unless you're reading it as an e-book, I want you to have it as a tangible tool you can use without a digital device beside you. As an offline tonic, you could say, to dip into whenever you need to rest, reflect and recharge, whatever the weather, inside or out.

In the main, I focus on self-devised retreats that you can do, in a space and place of your choosing, for an hour, a day, or longer. I also suggest ideas for the types of hosted, residential retreats available around the globe, related to relevant themes in each chapter, should you decide those are right for you (for more on hosted retreats, see Resources, p. 261).

I write this book as a journalist with more than thirty years' experience exploring retreats for international media, as the author of two 'healthy travel' guides, as the founder of a trusted retreat platform, and as a consultant who helps people create and improve retreats. I've also written it as someone who practices Yoga and Vedic Meditation every day, as a poet with faith in written words and the spaces between them, and as a mother, daughter, sister, wife, business partner and friend.

You'll discover practices in these pages that I have personally found to be the most effective over my three decades plus of retreating. Practices from retreats I have attended and written about, and those I have created for myself, inspired by the knowledge I've accumulated and the people I've met. That have become part of a personal toolkit, with which I reset myself as life ebbs and flows.

In one book I cannot hope to touch on every discipline out there. For every suggestion I make, there will be ten ideas I have missed, and emerging fields I've neglected to mention. But what I hope I've done is provide a framework for retreating, so that you can fill in the gaps with what works for you and go on to explore other pursuits and practices, creating your own personal journey of growth.

You'll find a little history, culture and science peppering these pages, to explain both where retreating practices come from and the connection between our brains and our bodies. Some, such as affirmations and reframing your limiting beliefs, work by helping us to rewire our neural pathways and experience neuroplasticity. This is the brain's remarkable ability to reorganise itself, by forming new neural connections in response to learning and experience (for more on this, see Resources, p. 261). But you'll also find the effects of retreating are experiential – that there's something intangible, even magical, about it that you'll only experience when you are actually on retreat.

Many people say many different things about how we should live – we're inundated. Some of this advice is often conflicting. *How To Retreat* is a book for individuals who don't want to be dictated to, but who want to follow their own path. So embrace what you find compelling and discard the rest. Listen to yourself. Go with your gut. Try new things. Be your own judge.

A word about emotional and mental stability

The practices in this book can be particularly helpful for anyone struggling with grief, loneliness, sadness, anxiety, depression, low self-esteem, insomnia, exhaustion, boredom and – let's face it – the general state of being human. It's important to note, however, that retreating is a prevention tool to enhance and maintain your wellbeing, not a cure if you are already feeling broken. It's like fixing a split tile in a roof while the sun is out, you could say, rather than waiting until they all fall off during a raging storm. This is why it's important to be mentally and emotionally stable when you retreat, especially on a self-devised retreat at home. If you are truly struggling, it's best to seek help from a trained doctor, counsellor or therapist before you start.

A word about poetry

I've scattered some quotations from literature throughout this book and referenced a few of my own poems that have emerged from retreating experiences (which you'll find in full in Retreat

Poems, p. 271). Reading and writing, especially poetry, have been my form of 'retreating' since I was a girl, way before I discovered retreats in any official sense. And I hope the retreats suggested in these pages will enable your own creative expression to flourish, in whatever way feels right for you, if it hasn't already done. To try your hand at writing a poem, see A Pause For Haiku, p. 113. For reading on retreats, see A Pause for Reading, p. 29.

Are you ready to retreat? Perhaps it's time to find out. Come on in. Your room is ready.

HOW TO USE THIS BOOK

How To Retreat is designed to make retreating available to you wherever you are in life. You can use it in three different ways:

- ✧ Choose the theme that resonates with you most right now, then retreat for an hour, a day, or longer, depending on how much time you have. Carry on dipping in and out of the book by theme as you feel the need.

- ✧ Follow the book chapter by chapter, theme by theme. Start with Purge, or whichever theme resonates with you most right now. Choose to retreat for an hour, a day, or longer, or engage with all three retreats one after the other.

- ✧ Start with the season you are in and follow the themes one by one as a seasonal roadmap, doing whichever retreats you can in the time you have (see Retreating by season, p. 13).

You'll find these three options in each chapter:

- **Retreat for an hour:** These are quick, immersive retreat practices that are ideal if you are short of time. When you have mastered them, they are easy to draw on in your daily life, whenever you need time out. They can also be made part of the longer self-devised retreats in this book when you get into the swing of things.

- **Retreat for a day:** These are ways to give yourself a meaningful day off that's easily slotted into a busy life. You'll be surprised what you can achieve in 24 hours, with the right preparation and intention. If you like a retreat theme and want to take more than a day to explore it, feel free to do so.

- **Retreat for longer:** These retreat ideas are for those craving something more intense, and who have more need and more time. They usually last two, three or five days, but you can, of course, make them longer than I have suggested. With some, there's also the option to do them in one-day batches, over a period of time, rather than all in one go.

However you choose to retreat, read Your Retreat Toolkit (p. 15) first and refer to it whenever you need throughout your retreats. Note that there are no set rules, and you can't do anything 'wrong'.

Happy retreating!

RETREATING BY SEASON

If we want them to, our retreat practices can shift with the seasons, each of which offers its own focus. Spring invites us to cleanse and declutter body and mind, and reconnect with ourselves, nature and community. Summer encourages us to embrace creativity and nurture ourselves with delight. Autumn teaches us to trust, reclaim our energy and build ourselves up, ready for Winter, which is a time to rest and recover, gather resolve and plan ahead.

YOUR RETREAT TOOLKIT

This toolkit is here to help you shape a retreat that feels both nourishing and enjoyable, whatever your circumstances or the time you have to spare. Settle in with a favourite soothing drink as you read, and return to these pages whenever you feel the need for guidance or inspiration.

Your toolkit includes:

How To Prepare For Your Retreat

- ✧ Choose the right time to retreat
- ✧ Choose who you will retreat with
- ✧ Give yourself permission to retreat
- ✧ Make a commitment to yourself
- ✧ Choose your retreat space

- ✧ Get your space retreat-ready
- ✧ Create a retreat stash

How To Structure Your Retreat

- ✧ Intention setting
- ✧ Retreat rituals
- ✧ Rest and movement breaks
- ✧ Suggested retreat schedule

How To Enrich Your Retreat

- ✧ Retreat nourishment
- ✧ Retreat journalling
- ✧ Embracing silence
- ✧ Digital resistance
- ✧ Surprise and delight
- ✧ Retreat reflection
- ✧ Continuing a retreat practice

How To Prepare For Your Retreat

Before you retreat, there are some useful things you can do to ensure you make the most of the experience. Think through what you will need and organise everything ahead of time, so that you can stay present and focus on your process.

Choose the right time to retreat

Choose a time for your retreat when you don't have any social engagements scheduled, and when you're in a quiet period for work and/or family life. Try to leave some space to relax and process either side of your retreat, whether it's an hour, a day, or more. For longer retreats in particular, plan a gentle run-up to it and a gentle restart back into daily life.

If you are a natural late sleeper or crave a lie-in, factor this in to your plan. If you want to do a day-long retreat, for example, you might plan to start your retreat at lunchtime and not finish it until lunchtime the following day, so you still get your 24 hours of retreat time without sleeping it all away.

If you are particularly time-pressed with family, work or other commitments, start small with the hour-long practices in this book. Build up to a day, a weekend, then longer retreats as your life allows. Over time you might retreat more regularly, as and when you need, peppering your year with retreat slots to enrich your life at different stages, based on what you're going through.

Choose who you will retreat with

RETREATING ALONE

For most people, the best way to retreat in a space of your choosing is to be alone. That way, you can truly focus on yourself and your needs, and get the most out of the process. Many retreat practices help you break free from the masks and labels we usually present to the world, and are a lot more effective if you are solo. They help you truly to be yourself without being self-conscious. Some can also make us grumpy for a short time, and these moods pass more quickly if we aren't bringing them into other people's lives and creating drama.

Avoiding interaction with others and the busy outside world is also part of the quietening down that retreating requires of you (see Go into silence, p. 208). The exception is when such interaction is intentional, such as a creative class or treatment session you might book as part of your retreat of choice, or a mindful sharing with a friend or family member at the end of a retreat day.

Finding time alone as a partner: If you live with a partner, but are choosing to retreat alone at home and have limited space, you might choose a time to retreat when they are going away, or ask them to consider going off to have their own adventure while you have yours. Another time, you can repay the favour, so that they can have some solo time to retreat too.

Finding time alone as a parent or carer: If you are a parent, make the most of when your children or teenagers are away on school trips, summer camps or student-led expeditions. Block out your calendar in advance with a retreat for yourself, rather than allowing the time to disappear in a sea of chores and admin.

If you look after younger children or older relatives, you might feel that taking just one hour entirely to yourself is more precious than trying to achieve more and getting stressed about it. But if you want to retreat for a day or longer, you could share the responsibility for looking after your dependants with a partner or another family member while you each take some time alone. Perhaps one person takes the mornings and the other the afternoons, or you each have a day, weekend or a longer period to yourselves?

It's wise not to experiment with new childcare during a retreat, if possible – opt for someone you know is reliable, and whom the children enjoy being with. You could also consider asking your partner, extended family or a trusted friend to take your children away for a few days on an adventure of their own while you retreat, then repay the favour another time and encourage them to have their own retreat time too. As every parent will tell you, there's something different about having your own house to yourself when everyone is out. Even just 24 hours of space and time to reflect can make a huge difference.

Managing shared spaces: If you live alone, retreating at home can be easier. If you live with others, such as family or housemates, but want to retreat alone while they are at home, discuss how this will work in advance. Where will you retreat, and how will you manage the logistics? Are you able to go somewhere else? (see Choose your retreat space, p. 22). If not, let others in your household know about your boundaries, and ask them gently for minimal interruptions.

Is there somewhere you can eat alone, if you would like to? Might someone cook your meals for you, and then you can repay the favour after your retreat? Sharing meals can be a lovely way to download in the evenings, but bear in mind your tribe are unlikely to be in the same state of mind as you. If they've not had a good day, for instance, you're likely to feel pulled in to pep them up and help, when what you really want to do is eat slowly in peace and quiet, and then go to bed. Take some time before you retreat to think about what would work best for you.

RETREATING WITH OTHERS

It can be enriching, powerful and connecting to share a longer retreat with one other person, such as your partner, a family member you get on well with, or a trusted friend. This needs to be done mindfully and with intention, however, to make the retreat worthwhile for both of you.

Retreating with another adult: Plan with intention to ensure you are each making the most of the retreat for your own sakes, and not having to 'look after' each other. Plan alone time into the schedule, so you can process and connect by yourselves. Declutter your stuff (p. 58), Garden (p. 74), Be kind (p. 82), Find your flow (p. 100), Treat yourself (p. 126), Stay put (p. 134), Unplug (p. 177) and, possibly, Re-imagine your life (p. 235) could all work well with someone else. Whatever you choose, set the intention to be kind to one another during your retreat, and to stay flexible with your schedules.

Retreating with teenagers: Some of the retreat practices in this book are suitable for mature teenagers, and it can be delightful to do this with them as a parent. They might particularly relish and benefit from Declutter your stuff (p. 58), Be kind (p. 82), Find your flow (p. 100), Embody (p. 119), Choose gratitude (p. 146), De-excite (p. 163), Unplug (p. 177), Be mindful (p. 199) and Design your day (p. 221).

Retreating with your willing teenager can be a powerful experience, during which you could help each other thrive and deepen the connection between you. A daily structure is particularly helpful. Get up and go to bed at the same time each morning and evening. Plan to have some time together and alone. Make healthy meals together. Go for long walks.

Retreating with children: You could invite your younger children into a creative or active part of your retreat practice. They might relish some of the activities, for example, in Garden (p. 74), Find your flow (p. 100) or Be an artist (p. 108). If you choose to retreat by staying put together for a longer time, children can also be factored into your schedule and activities. You'll know what works best for you and your brood. Whatever you choose, a family-focused retreat is a great time to let go of any perfectionism around parenting. Set the intention to simply go with the flow, free of any 'shoulds'.

Give yourself permission to retreat

When you are ready, give yourself permission to retreat. We are all brilliant at finding reasons why we should not, but put aside your guilt, your busyness and your excuses. Encourage significant others to do so too. It's easy to believe that we haven't got the resources we might need, but retreating doesn't have to be time consuming, extreme or expensive. We can create the right conditions if we want to, by shifting something here, prioritising there and gathering support from those around us. Know that retreating helps us *create* more time, space and energy for life, rather than taking those things away. To press pause and regroup *before* we reach breaking point, so we can return to our daily lives with more of what we need for ourselves, our family, our work and any other commitments we may have.

Make a commitment to yourself

A retreat isn't a passive experience, like, for example, staying somewhere on holiday can be. If you commit to bringing your whole self to it, without distraction, you are more likely to get what you need and want out of it. This is especially the case when you are on a self-devised retreat in a space of your choosing. So whether you have time to retreat for an hour, a day, or longer, and alone or with another, make a commitment by writing, or saying aloud, something like: 'I commit to giving this retreat my time and energy, my full presence and attention.' Once you have done so, block out the time you have chosen in your calendar and label it RETREAT. Hold your course. You'll see that it's worth it when you do.

Choose your retreat space

The space you choose to retreat in is an essential element to its success, and it needs to feel delightful. Having a calm, comfortable and private space that's just for you will help you relax and fully engage with the experience, especially when you are on a self-devised retreat. Where will you retreat for your hour, day, weekend or longer period of time? This might well change from retreat to retreat.

For an hour: Find a quiet, private space anywhere you can sit comfortably. This could be inside your home but it could also be in a quiet corner of your office, a hotel room, a gallery, museum or church, a library, in a room in the house of a friend you trust, or even in a park on a still and sunny day. You might already have a daily resting place where you know you will go. Switching off all your devices quickly turns anywhere you are into a retreat (see p. 37). Wherever you choose, use a ritual to honour the space before you begin (see p. 26).

For a day, weekend, or longer: Your own home may already be a haven for you, or you may have a haven within it. Otherwise, you could create one in your bedroom, a spare room, or an area of your sitting room or home office. You may have your whole home at your disposal, or just one discreet area. Perhaps you have a garden or other outside space you can retreat to, such as a bell tent, camper van, shed or studio you can call your own, if only for a short while.

If you feel it would be easier to retreat in a different space to your home, and to be away from everything, consider alternatives. You might like an anonymous space, without your personal belongings, where you have a blank canvas on which to recreate yourself. You could rent a room in a hotel, guesthouse or B&B, or a self-catering studio, flat, cabin, cottage, house, villa or other property in a location that appeals to you. The geographical area you choose could have personal significance for you – perhaps somewhere you went as a child and remember with joy, for example. It could even be just up the road from where you live now, for ease. If budget is a concern, retreating off season can make this much more affordable than you might think. You could also use a space in a good friend's house, or do a home swap.

Get your space retreat-ready

When you have chosen your space, clean, tidy and prepare it to retreat in. Imagine you have arrived at a hosted retreat and opened the door of your room. What would you like to find, and how would you like to feel? Aim to replicate that in your chosen place.

Remember that you don't have to spend money to create nurturing spaces. Often one simple thing can lift it. For example, as writer, poet and gardener Vita Sackville-West put it in her book *In Your Garden*: 'a flowerless room is a soul-less room, to my thinking; but even one solitary little vase of a living flower may redeem it.'

Think through areas where you will move and rest, write and create, plan and ponder, eat and sleep, and turn each of them into a sanctuary. Whether you like a decluttered space or prefer to have creature comforts nearby, the key thing is to make it yours, and somewhere you can settle and focus.

You might have fresh flowers, an inspiring artwork or framed picture that feels suited to you right now, a stash of books, or cushions for comfort and colour. Have a blanket or shawl to hand, perhaps, because when we start to relax, let go and process, we can often get chilly. Consider laying your table with a clean cloth before your meals, even though – or especially because – it may only be you eating.

Re-set wherever you'll be sleeping, so that it's a place you can lie down whenever you need, or, alternatively, choose a different place for daytime rest, such as a hammock in the garden or your sofa. Create your own 'turn down service' for the evenings too. Organise fresh bedding and nightwear before your retreat starts. Consider having lavender essential oil or a sleep spray ready for your pillow.

It's a good idea to air your retreat space daily, by opening a window wide for a few minutes before you begin, and to keep a window ajar while you retreat. Fresh air improves focus, mental clarity and mood, helping you think, create and relax more effectively. Have water to hand in a flask or jug as well, with a mug or glass it's a pleasure to drink from. Ideally, make the water warm (see p. 34).

Remember, too, that nature is your space, whether that's your own garden, a local park, a stretch of beach or a nearby woodland trail. Which outside spaces might you use as part of your retreat?

Dealing with chores: Before your retreat starts, tidy, clean, do laundry and take care of any necessary domestic or administrative tasks. This way, you won't see a 'to do list' in every corner while you are retreating, and you'll be able to enjoy some chore-free time. For a longer retreat at home, you could make any light tasks that help you feel comfortable in your space part of a quiet morning routine. Then, at the end of each retreat day, tidy your retreat space for a sense of closure.

Create a retreat stash

What you put in your chosen retreat space matters. Consider assigning a special, secret box, drawer, cupboard or holdall in your home where you can stash things that will help you feel nurtured and charmed on your retreat of choice. It can be as small or as big as you choose, and filled with anything that works for you. If you're intending to go away for a self-devised retreat, or to go on a hosted retreat at a later date, you could take the most portable things in your stash with you.

Your retreat stash could include: a precious object that has meaning for you; a favourite piece of jewellery or scarf to wear only when you retreat; a quote or picture that resonates with you; a fresh notebook and a favourite pen or pencil; art materials;

a shawl, warm socks and hot water bottle to keep you cosy; a decorated flask or a distinctive glass or cup for drinks; a favourite book to read in your retreat breaks; a special pillowcase you keep only for retreating; a fragrant candle of your choice with a lighter; downloaded music and guided meditations for evening rituals; essential oils for your pulse points, such as lavender, rose or bergamot; natural oils for self-massage, such as coconut or almond; a box of tissues; a note of kindness, encouragement or humour to yourself.

How to Structure Your Retreat

Giving your retreat a structure will help you stay relaxed, focused and productive. Once you have chosen which retreat you want to do, you can structure it by setting an intention for it, picking rituals to anchor it, adding rest and movement breaks, and creating a light schedule to follow.

Intention setting

Setting a personal intention before each retreat helps to bring clarity and purpose to it. It turns it into a complete practice, and helps us be fully present in, and open to, the experience that is about to unfold.

To set an intention:

- ✧ **Take a moment:** Check in with yourself and reflect on what you need: What do you want to get out of this retreat? What do you need in your life right now? What do you want more (or less) of? What emotions or experiences are you hungry for?

- ✧ **Keep it simple and positive:** Your intention can be anything you choose, but intentions work best when they're clear, affirming and realistic. Examples might be:

'On this retreat I will allow myself to rest deeply', or 'on this retreat I will allow myself to create freely and without judging myself', and so on.

- **Write it down or say it aloud:** Journalling or speaking your intention makes it more powerful. You can also revisit it throughout the retreat as a reminder.

- **Connect with it emotionally:** Visualise what it feels like to live out your intention. Let that feeling guide your choices and actions during your retreat. Don't set the bar too high. Be gentle on yourself.

- **Release the outcome:** We can't predict what will happen, and what we planned for might not happen, but we can set our intentions. Unlike expectations, which can be thwarted, or goals, which focus on results, intentions are about the present moment. Set it, embody it, then let it go and trust the process.

Retreat rituals

Rituals are simple, short practices that can create anchors in your daily life. On a retreat, they serve as gentle transitions, helping you begin and end a retreat task or day with intention, grace and good humour. The trick is to pick small, consistent acts that cultivate mindfulness and create a sense of calm and purpose. If you find one you really like, it can become part of your regular self-care.

To begin a retreat hour or a distinct retreat task: You could place a treasured object, some flowers in a vase or something from nature close by you, just to signify to yourself that you are on retreat. Using an essential oil of your choice on your pulse points can also help to set a calming, focused tone before you begin. If you are at home, you could light a candle.

To begin and end a retreat day: For each retreat that lasts a day or longer, pick daily morning and evening rituals that resonate with you. Done soon after waking, they help you arrive fully into your day. Nearing sleep, they help you unwind meaningfully at the day's close. You could start with some of the ideas below, but, over time, feel free to let the right rituals unfold for you.

MORNING RITUAL IDEAS

- Bring to mind one thing you are grateful for today. It could be something simple that you're experiencing in the moment, such as the sunshine coming through your window, or something more intricate and personal to you that you plan to do.

- Go outside barefoot or stand at an open window and take ten slow deep breaths of fresh air, in through your nose and out through your mouth.

- Listen to one piece of exceptional music that grounds you.

- Make your bed with care.

EVENING RITUAL IDEAS

- Mentally 'shelve' three good moments from your day. Picture a small shelf beside you. Place three moments from the day on it – something that was amusing, inspiring, kind, clever or quiet, perhaps? – before you turn out the light.

- Massage your head, feet or hands slowly and mindfully with a natural oil.

- Read a comforting or calming short passage or poem.

- Give yourself a quiet 'inner weather report'. Close your eyes and notice what the weather feels like inside you tonight – a little cloudy, bright and breezy, calm or changeable? Name it gently.

Rest and movement breaks

Whatever your chosen theme, take at least 30 minutes away from the proposed retreat activity each morning and afternoon. This will allow you to subconsciously process your experiences and replenish your resources. Call this a 'break' on your schedule, then decide on the day whether you will rest or move. Ensure at least one of your breaks is outside, for a mood lift closer to nature.

Usually, you'd schedule movement in the morning and rest in the afternoon, but listen to your body. Retreating is about honouring yourself, not 'pushing through' as you might do in another life or work situation. If you are tired, rest, even if you have just got up. If you are restless or have been static for too long, move instead, even if it's the evening. It's that simple.

Resting: Rest on a retreat isn't complicated. Simply stop what you are doing and do something you like that feels restful instead. What might this be? Different things work for different people. It might be reading (see A Pause For Reading below) or weeding, doing nothing in particular, lying down somewhere comfy with your eyes closed, meditating, daydreaming, playing an instrument, listening to music, doodling or sketching. If you don't allow yourself to truly rest very often, experiment with a few things until you find what works.

A PAUSE FOR READING

Reading is one of the simplest ways to take a restful break on a retreat. The right book carries you into flow, so that nothing else matters and time disappears (see Find your flow, p. 100). It takes you on a journey without leaving home, giving your mind relief from its own concerns, and can feel deeply restorative. It provides solace, comfort and interest.

Reading also connects you to others and reflects you back to yourself. That moment when a line makes you think, 'Yes, that's me' helps you feel less alone. It lowers stress, improves focus and invites the mind to soften. You can read fully absorbed, or pause between pages, drift, gaze out of a window, or simply breathe the air – it's all part of resting where you are.

Choose what you read with care. Just as food shapes the body, what you read shapes your mind and wellbeing. This isn't the time for horror or heavy news. Though only you know what soothes you. Autobiographies about people's experience of being in silence, accessible Buddhist writings about the human condition, timeless novels and short stories can work well. Well-chosen, relatable poems or song lyrics can also offer us comfort or connection within a short space of time.

Reading in this way becomes bibliotherapy – a self-devised medicine for our hearts and minds. Which is why there's a scattering of hosted reading retreats around the globe. For ideas for books to retreat with, see Resources, p. 261.

Moving: Movement that gets your heartrate up is essential for our physical and mental health, especially when you are on retreat and have chosen to focus on looking after yourself. Be intentional about how and when you are going to move, and listen to your body. You might like to walk (see A Pause For Walking below), run, cycle, swim, dance or something else instead. Make it easy, something you can do with minimal equipment, and if you're moving outside, from the door of wherever your retreat is taking place, so you don't have to travel.

Note that movement on retreat is not 'exercise' per se. We live in a pushy world, where society is usually telling us to do more, speed up, go faster, tone this and that. A retreat is a chance to step away from that pressure. Doing a round of weights or circuits, say, or rebounding on a mini trampoline, are both totally valid for your movement slot if they make you feel good. But don't move vigorously if you are depleted – rest instead.

A PAUSE FOR WALKING

Walking makes an ideal choice of break while you are on retreat, because it functions as a form of both rest and movement. It can be done straight from your door and it costs nothing. It both boosts your mood and works out your body. It also allows your subconscious to process your thoughts and feelings, safely and steadily, especially after an intense retreat practice.

Whether you're doing an easy circular walk, strolling on a beach, rambling across countryside or ambling through your local park, walk just fast enough to increase your heart rate and let your arms swing free. Walking methodically, without the pressure of 'getting somewhere', is a meditation. A way to shut up a chattering mind and refresh yourself, where you might have felt stressed or stale before.

Brisk walking in fresh air, natural light and open landscapes also clears the head, improves brainpower and boosts concentration, which is why writers and philosophers from Aristotle to Wordsworth walked regularly to help them think and create.

The nineteenth-century existentialist Danish philosopher Søren Kierkegaard captures the benefits of walking brilliantly in a letter he wrote to his niece, Henriette Lund, in 1847: 'Above all, do not lose your desire to walk,' he advises her. 'Every day I walk myself into a state of well-being and walk away from every illness. I have walked myself into my best thoughts, and I know of no thought so burdensome that one cannot walk away from it.'

Suggested retreat schedule

If you are retreating for a day, a weekend, or longer, create a light retreat schedule beforehand that gives you enough space and time between activities to process, rest and move. *Light* is the key word here. Stay flexible, and be prepared to tweak it as your retreat unfolds. Don't be too concerned about timings (see Choose the right time to retreat, p. 17, for tips).

On a longer retreat, start with an idea of what your first day might look like, then go with your intuition and your energy. Of course, if your retreat of choice includes a treatment or class, you'll need to research and book them in advance so you can build your schedule around them.

Below is a suggested schedule. Feel free to copy the main headings out before each retreat, in your journal or on a fresh piece of paper, and change and personalise as you see fit. See Retreat nourishment (opposite) for ideas about what to eat and drink.

- **The evening before each retreat day:** Switch off and put away all distractions, including your electronic devices. Allow yourself a good night's sleep, and don't set an alarm, so you can let yourself wake naturally on your retreat day.

- **Morning ritual:** Best done on waking (see p. 27 for ideas).

- **Morning practice:** After your morning ritual is the time to do any regular practice you may have, such as Meditation or Yoga, to go for a short run or walk, or to simply move in a way that feels good to you. Let yourself arrive into your day retreat with awareness, and without rush. If you go out, avoid interactions.

- **Rise and nourish:** Wash and dress comfortably, then sustain yourself with breakfast.

- **Morning activities:** Begin the first few activities appropriate for the retreat you have chosen, usually lasting up to a few hours. On a longer retreat, your morning and afternoon activity could well be combined into one daytime activity.

- **Break and nourish:** Rest or move for 30 minutes or so, depending on what your body needs (see p. 28 for break ideas), before or after having lunch.

- **Afternoon activities:** Do the next few activities appropriate for the retreat you have chosen, taking as long as you want, and having breaks as you feel the need.

✧ **Break and nourish:** Rest or move for 30 minutes or so, depending on what your body needs (see p. 28 for break ideas), before having an evening meal.

✧ **Evening activities:** Do the final activities appropriate for the retreat you have chosen. Make sure you give yourself time and space for 'closure' afterwards.

✧ **Evening ritual:** Best done nearing bedtime (see p. 28 for ideas). Stay off digital media. Allow yourself to get to bed at a decent time. You are still on retreat.

✧ **The morning after a retreat:** Start as gently and slowly as you can. Delay switching your electronic devices back on for as long as possible.

How to Enrich Your Retreat

Retreat nourishment

What and how you eat and drink on retreat will help contribute to its success. As author Virginia Woolf noted in her call for a private space, *A Room of One's Own*: 'One cannot think well, love well, sleep well, if one has not dined well.'

Eating: While one of the joys of a hosted retreat is that someone else has planned and cooked your meals, nourishing yourself on a self-devised retreat doesn't have to be complicated or stressful. Before your retreat, plan some simple, tasty dishes and buy the ingredients, so you don't have to worry about shopping. You might consider batch cooking some meals in advance too. For recipe sources, see Resources, p. 261.

This is a good time to interrupt your usual habits and invite yourself to be curious about what you normally consume. Avoid refined sugar and ultra-processed foods. Use organic, seasonal and locally sourced ingredients where you can, for nutrients and flavour, and herbs and spices for taste.

You'll want to choose foods that support your body's needs and the energy requirements of the retreat theme you have chosen. Know that plants in particular are easy to digest, rich in fibre and antioxidants, support the liver and kidneys, reduce inflammation and help hydrate you too.

I suggest trying to make brunch or lunch on your retreat the main meal of the day, as this is when the digestive system is usually at its strongest. To give your system a rest and gift yourself the best chance of a good sleep, avoid eating large, heavy meals, and eating late in the evening. Make sitting down to every meal an enjoyable ritual, and eat consciously (see A Pause For Eating Consciously, opposite).

Drinking: Water, drunk regularly throughout the day, is the best thing to drink on retreats and throughout your life. Our brain is made up of 80 per cent water, and our bodies are between 45 to 75 per cent water, depending on our sex and age, yet most of us are dehydrated a lot of the time. Proponents of Ayurveda suggest that the body absorbs warm water more easily, and I personally find warm or hot water more calming and comforting at any time, especially on retreat. I boil a kettle each morning, fill a thermos flask, and carry this with me throughout my day. The key thing is to keep hydrated, whatever temperature you like your water.

To remain clear-headed, calm and able to focus, avoid all alcohol (and drugs) on your retreat, and be careful about how much caffeine you drink. A cup or two of white, black or green tea, or good coffee, drunk mindfully on a retreat day can be divine, but avoid having multiple cups and agitating your system.

Herbal teas or homemade tisanes made with herbs, flowers, roots and spices are refreshing alternatives to caffeinated drinks. Japanese root tea and red bush (Rooibos) tea make especially pleasing alternatives to coffee. Miso soup, which can be purchased in jars or sachets in supermarkets, is satisfying to sip at any time. For evening comfort, I love a turmeric latte: combine your milk of choice with a sprinkle of turmeric and a splash of honey or agave syrup, then warm up and whip until frothy.

A PAUSE FOR EATING CONSCIOUSLY

Canadian nutritionist Rebecca Andrist was the first person who taught me how to eat consciously on one of her inspired Jiva Healing retreats. Here are the tips I learned from her:

- **Don't eat when agitated:** If you eat while stressed, angry or generally irritated, your body focuses on those feelings instead of digestion, often leaving you tired and uncomfortable. Take five slow breaths before each meal to relax, and eat in a calm environment without screens or noise.

- **Don't eat in a rush:** Slow down when you eat, and don't eat on the move. Try putting your knife and fork down between mouthfuls to ensure you take your time.

- **Savour your food:** Taking your time to enjoy each bite helps you tune into your body's signals, and makes meals more enjoyable. Pleasure and relaxation while eating naturally boost digestion.

- **Eat to the point of energy, not fullness:** Follow the Japanese idea of 'Hara Hachi Bu', and stop eating when you're about 80 per cent full. Eating less

> helps digestion and leaves you with more energy for the things you love.

Retreat journalling

Journalling helps you pay attention to what matters on a retreat. Having a fresh notebook to write in can be a helpful way of keeping things in one place and working things through in your mind. You'll also have a record of things you have experienced for your future reference.

If this appeals to you, take some time and pleasure in finding the right notebook, and know that you're likely to get through a few of them if you get into the practice.

Don't feel too precious about your journal. See it as a space to explore and experiment. It's okay to cross out, write messily, draw and doodle, colour and highlight. If there are nuggets of truth that emerge that you want to keep moving forward, you could always copy them out into another book, add them to your own field guide (see Practise self-reliance, p. 152), or even display them.

Using a paper journal while you work through the retreats in this book makes things easy and keeps your notes all in one place, but it is optional. You might instead write in the 'journal' of your mind, simply 'thinking' about your reactions, or use a pad of loose paper. For more on journalling as a practice, see Journal, p. 69.

Embracing silence

Finding peace and quiet, both within us and without, is a significant part of what a retreat is all about. You'll find that things naturally quieten as you slow down, tune out the outside world and tune into yourself. You won't have to be in total silence to thrive, but there are things you can do to enhance this inner settling and to discourage unnecessary noise.

As you go about your day, establish your own quietude. Choose silence, rather than listening to something, first thing each morning. Eat, drink, create, move, rest and journal in relative quiet. Be mindful what you choose to say, read and listen to, so you don't invite agitation. We can gently talk, or listen to wonderful music, in a way that benefits us. We can still say 'thank you' or 'hello' if we encounter someone, but we can resist stopping for a chat.

Some hosted retreats add explicit periods of silence to their programmes. They might suggest there is no talking before or during breakfast, on a walk each day, or during afternoon downtime, to allow guests to resist mindless chatter, calm down and tune into themselves. You might like to replicate this, especially if you are on a retreat for longer than a day and live with others, or if you are retreating with someone else. Silence can be delicious and magical rather than something to be afraid of – for more on this, see Go into silence, p. 208.

Digital resistance

The quickest, most powerful way to bring a nourishing silence into your retreat is simply to unplug all your electronic devices for the duration. It's all part of turning down the 'noise' in your life, both literally and figuratively, so you can focus on yourself and the retreat's activities.

Before your retreat hour: Simply switch off all your digital devices and put them away.

For your retreat day: Check digital media in the early evening the day before, then switch off all electronic devices entirely a few hours before bed and put them away in a room you don't plan to use during your retreat day. Keep them there for the duration of your retreat day and evening, so you can intentionally stay present. Only access them again, and ideally not first thing, the morning after your retreat day – most things can wait until then.

For a longer retreat: I would also encourage a total digital detox for a retreat that lasts longer than a day, but if you can't disengage from things entirely, choose how and when you will access any electronic devices before you begin. You could give yourself just one set time each day to engage digitally where necessary, for example. Up to an hour before your evening meal may work. Avoid all unnecessary scrolling, and only stick to important tasks. Vow to switch off until the same time the following day.

TIPS FOR STAYING OFFLINE WHILE YOU RETREAT

- If you find it difficult to stay off your electronic devices, consider giving them to a family member, neighbour or friend the evening before your retreat starts, and pledge not to ask for them back until the morning after your retreat ends.

- Tell friends and family you will be offline and not contactable except in emergencies. Plan ahead for what matters, so that another parent or trusted friend is the main contact for your children, for example, or you have access to a phone that is only for phone calls.

- To listen to music, podcasts or meditations during retreat activities or breaks, find a way to do so that doesn't require a phone or internet connection. You might have a CD or record player, or you could maybe download what you need onto a portable offline music player.

- To tell the time during your retreats, buy or borrow an analogue portable or wall clock. Or why not just forget about the time for this short while?

- To take photographs for retreat activities, buy or borrow an offline camera, such as a disposable, polaroid or SLR model.

- To make notes, use your journal or a pad of loose paper. Write your schedules on paper, and consider switching to a paper diary for the duration of your retreating.

- If you need to use your smartphone to listen to things, tell the time, take photos, make notes or access your calendar, set the intention to keep the notifications off, and put your settings into Airplane Mode.

- Anticipate that switching off may feel challenging, even boring, and plan your boundaries ahead of time. Unplugging can be tricky, but it's one of the loveliest things to do to regain our attention for what matters. To do it as a dedicated retreat, and for more information, see Unplug, p. 177.

Surprise and delight

Every good retreat has an element of surprise and delight – to refresh and motivate you, give you joy, or inspire you to revisit shelved dreams. Ask yourself, what makes you feel delight? When you're retreating in a space of your choosing, consider ways to create this for yourself. Decorating your retreat space with things that uplift and nurture you is an easy win (see p. 23). The trick is to help yourself feel special.

One idea is to create themed jars in advance, one for every room, which you can open and browse at random during your retreat. Each could be filled with: quotes you love; jokes; pictures or phrases of things to do, or places to visit; names of songs or pieces of music to play; praise and confidence boosts you have received, and copied out, from different people in your life; things and people you appreciate (see Choose gratitude, p. 146); things you trust (see self-trust jars in Practise self-reliance, p. 152).

If you're retreating with someone else, you could create a personalised retreat treasure hunt for each other, leaving clues in sealed envelopes that lead to small surprises such as a poem, tasty snack or tiny craft item. Tuck hand-written notes of kindness, praise or pressed flowers inside a book they are reading, for example, or under their pillow – or why not do the same for yourself?

Simply being open to what might happen on your retreat may be enough. Not taking ourselves too seriously, and seeing the humour in a situation, might be another.

Retreat reflection

After a retreat, it's wise to take a short time to reflect on your experience, so you can better harness any insights and let them positively influence your mindset, emotions and actions once you return to your regular routines. Each retreat in this book includes prompts to help with this process.

Please remember that this is an ongoing journey, one that happens at different paces for different people. Allow things to unfold naturally and be patient with yourself. Sharing your reflections with your journal, a trusted friend, family member or community can often deepen your understanding and growth.

Continuing a retreat practice

At the end of each retreat, I've suggested ways you can extend the practice if you so choose, turning it into a longer-term way of seeing or being, for the benefit of both yourself and your life. You'll also find ideas for hosted, residential retreats to attend that relate to the theme, where relevant (for more on hosted retreats, see Resources, p. 261).

Once you get into the swing of retreating, why not schedule a regular retreat hour for yourself each week, a retreat day each month, and one or two longer retreats each year of your life? Draw on what you have liked most, using notes you have taken, to create a way of retreating that suits you.

PRE-RETREAT CHECKLISTS

For your ease, use these checklists to help you plan each retreat.

Before all retreats

✧ Choose your time and date, block it out as a RETREAT in your calendar and commit to it.

✧ Read the section for your chosen retreat all the way through, writing a list of any materials you might need as you do so.

✧ Pick your activities, if there is a choice.

✧ Choose and prepare your retreat space.

✧ Set an intention that feels right for you.

Just before your retreat hour

✧ We are most open to change, suggestion and creativity when we are in a serene state, so do something that helps you relax before your hour begins, whether that's going for a short walk, having a shower, settling yourself with a cup of tea or something else equally conducive to a state of serenity.

✧ Have to hand water to drink, your journal or loose paper with a pen or pencil, and whatever you have chosen to help you ritualise your retreat hour.

✧ Switch off and put away all distractions and electronic devices.

One week or more before a day or longer retreat

✧ Choose to retreat alone or who you will retreat with. Discuss how your retreat will work, if you share your space, and alert anyone who needs to know if/how you will be contactable.

- ✧ Gather any materials you need, including your journal or loose paper with a pen or pencil.

- ✧ Plan and shop for what you will eat and drink; batch cook in advance if you need.

- ✧ Choose your morning and evening rituals, your rest and movement breaks, and devise a light, personal schedule.

- ✧ Switch off and put away all electronic devices for the duration, or set boundaries for when you will engage with them.

PURGE

'Starting today I will exfoliate my regrets'
Theresa Lola, 'To My Previous Self'

Is your mind stacked with confusing thoughts, your body sluggish, your desk a mess? Purging our minds, bodies and homes while on retreat can help us re-enter life refreshed and recharged, and ready to truly live.

To purge – from the Latin *pūrgāre*, meaning 'to purify' – is to remove anything unwanted, whether it's noisy thoughts, negative energy or physical clutter. Throughout history, people have embraced ways to purge what no longer serves them, from water fasting and spring cleaning to cultural and religious rituals that help them let go of old habits and beliefs.

What do you need to let go of? Sometimes you might need to shed a lot, including emotional baggage. At other times, small practices of sorting and freshening can ground and invigorate us for whatever lies ahead.

How much time do you have to retreat?

- ✧ An hour – Clear your mind (p. 47)
- ✧ A day – Refresh yourself (p. 51)
- ✧ Longer – Declutter your stuff (p. 58)

Whatever you choose, refer to the Retreat Toolkit (p. 15) to help you prepare for each retreat.

Start with a check-in

Write in your journal or think to yourself:

- ✧ *An old, familiar story about myself I tell others over and over is . . .*
- ✧ *I have the most energy when . . .*
- ✧ *The space in my house, garden or office I'd most like to clear out is . . . because . . .*

RETREAT FOR AN HOUR
CLEAR YOUR MIND

Do you wake up, or go to bed, or have periods in the middle of your day, when your psyche feels packed full of agitating thoughts, feelings and worries? Taking pen to paper can be an effective way to offload the low-energy noise and nonsense that floats around at the top of our minds, so that we can begin again, afresh and free.

Morning Pages, for example, is a powerful writing practice devised by Julia Cameron in her book *The Artist's Way*. Described as 'three pages of longhand, stream of consciousness morning writing about absolutely anything', it's one of the most effective techniques I've learned on a retreat to help clear mind clutter on waking and begin each day with creativity and intention.

In the evenings, or if I wake in the middle of the night, I'll write a Worry List instead of fretting, getting anything that's agitating or annoying me out of my mind and onto paper, to deal with tomorrow. Or if I'm in the middle of the day and my brain feels full, I'll simply write for as long as I need to, filling pages with ramblings until I feel released.

Clearing your thoughts in any of these ways is not the same as journalling, however, which is a conscious, explorative way of connecting with where you are in your day and your life (see Journal, p. 69). These are not pages you need to re-read, or to show anyone else, and, afterwards, you can recycle, burn or just hide them away.

Take an hour to offload on paper

When your brain is feeling over full, at any time of day, take an hour to release your mental cacophony onto the page. Pick a pen or pencil you like, loose paper or a notebook that's different to your regular journal if you have one, then simply write, without censoring yourself.

If it's first thing in the morning: On waking, do Julia Cameron's Morning Pages, for which you write three pages, no more and no less, about anything at all. You'll be surprised how long this can take. If you get to the third page and feel frustrated, with nothing to say, just write anything, such as, 'this is a struggle, filling this page, I am not sure what to write, later at my desk I will tackle that difficult email' and so on. Carrying on, even when you don't want to, ensures your mind gets a total clear-out. You might find, too, like I often do, that you end up delving into a subject that was clearly bothering you underneath the surface.

If you finish quickly, don't be tempted to write any more. Instead, pay attention to what's come into your brain – sometimes it might be your to do list for the day, or your shopping list for later. You might even have found clarity on an issue with which you were struggling. Make any notes you need on a separate piece of paper. Spend the rest of your hour doing something simple and mindful, such as making and enjoying a cup of tea.

If it's the middle of the day: Write free-flow, getting any anxiety, anger and angst out onto the page. This is especially good if you are feeling jaded and fed up. Moving your body with a short walk or by dancing, before or after you write, will help you process too.

If it's the evening or night: Write a Worry List, noting down in brief form anything stressful you need to deal with tomorrow or another time, so you don't have to concern yourself with it now. Afterwards, do a gentle body scan to settle yourself (see De-excite, p. 163).

Enjoy the rest of your day, or go to sleep, with a clearer mind.

Tips for a successful practice

- ✧ In the morning or in the middle of the day, know there is no wrong or right way to offload. Just write anything and everything that crosses your mind, from desires and regrets to dreams and lists, to inane comments or profound poetic lines.

- ✧ The evening or the middle of the night isn't the time to write a lot – that will only agitate you more. This is why it's a worry *list*, rather than an extended account of your thoughts and feelings.

- ✧ Whenever you write to offload, you'll often find useful, practical things come to mind, such as essentials you need to buy. Write them down on a separate piece of paper to ease your mental load.

Reflect on your practice

Ask yourself later that day, how did you feel after writing out your worries and woes? Was there relief, resistance, or a shift in energy or clarity? Try the process again over the next few days and see what the effect is, and if it changes or evolves.

Continue your practice

Offloading on paper is an easy addition in your life. Take some blank paper and a pencil with you wherever you go. Julia

Cameron designed her Morning Pages to be done daily over a period of time. Play with what works for you. You might, like me, find them particularly useful when working through change, or on an innovative project.

RETREAT FOR A DAY
REFRESH YOURSELF

What does refreshment mean to you? A cool drink, an invigorating shower, a bracing swim in the sea, a siesta? Waking ourselves up, and releasing gloominess and tension, doesn't have to be complicated. Throughout history, the notion of refreshment has been intricately tied to simple yet profound acts of renewal that we can also draw on in our daily lives.

Drinking and bathing in water are the oldest, most universal forms of refreshment. From the holy waters of the Ganges to 'taking the waters' at Roman public baths, and the communal steam rooms of Turkish hammams, these rituals went beyond quenching thirst or cleaning the body, to hold symbolic meanings of purification and restoration.

Ancient civilisations complemented their bathing with other acts of self-care, such as dry body brushing – practised since ancient Egyptian times to stimulate circulation and refresh the senses – and tongue scraping, rooted in Ayurveda and used to improve oral hygiene as well as refresh the breath. Cultures of all kinds have historically scrubbed their bodies with loofahs, mitts and natural exfoliating ingredients, such as salt, oils and herbs, to gently remove dead skin but also to invite in new vitality.

Paired with time spent moving freely in nature, and honouring the restorative sanctuary of sleep, such rituals form part of a holistic cycle of refreshment we can use to meet our needs. If your body feels sluggish, your mind heavy, and you're carrying around a whole heap of negative energy, taking a day to refresh yourself might be just the ticket.

Take a day to revive body and mind

This is an easy retreat day, and something to do if you're not feeling up to much. Plan a personal, pleasurable schedule of invigorating rituals and activities that takes you from morning to night. Gather the materials you might need in advance – you can buy body brushes and tongue scrapers from most health shops, for example.

Suggested schedule

On waking: Start your day with a cleansing mug of hot water, laced with a generous squeeze of fresh lemon and lots of chopped root ginger. Give the ginger time to steep. Drinking this first thing helps us boost immunity and reduce inflammation, thanks to the vitamin C and antioxidants in lemon, and the anti-inflammatory compounds in ginger. Then take your journal or some loose paper and offload all the noise in your brain onto the page (see Clear your mind, p. 47).

Morning: Get up and take time to immerse yourself in cleansing body rituals that appeal to you. You might do one or all of these:

- **Brush your skin:** Brush your skin all over with a body brush to wake yourself up, stimulate your lymphatic system and boost circulation. Start with your feet and move up your body, brushing in upward strokes.

- **Clean your tongue:** Brush your teeth methodically and for longer than usual. Then use your toothbrush, or a tongue scraper if you have one, to clean your tongue properly. This removes the bacteria and debris that cause bad breath, improves your sense of taste and supports your oral health.

- **Prolong your shower:** Have a shower, then turn the temperature to cool, and as you do so, mimic the ancient Japanese ritual of Misogi. This is where practitioners stand under a waterfall for purification, using the intense experience for renewal and mindfulness. Stand under your cool shower for a good few minutes or more, making it gradually colder if you can. Focus on the sensation of moving water and cold, using the moment to let go of stress. Turn the water back to warm for a few moments before you get out.

- **Scrub your body:** Scrub your arms, legs and body with an exfoliating scrub to remove dead skin cells, unclog pores, boost circulation, and soften and smooth your skin. Work from your feet and move upwards, then rinse off.

  To make your own scrub, mix raw cane sugar or sea salt with coconut, olive or almond oil, and a few drops of an essential oil of your choice for fragrance. Or there are plenty of ready-made scrubs available – go for something that has a use by date, though, so you know it's been made with fresh, natural ingredients.

When you have finished your body rituals, dry yourself, get dressed, have a sustaining breakfast and make yourself a healthy packed lunch, ready for an excursion.

Mid morning: There are few more energising, head-clearing and mood-boosting things to do than being active in the elements, so take yourself on an outdoor adventure that involves moving in nature.

You could:

- Go swimming in a clean local lake, river, loch or the sea to clear your head, soothe aching muscles, boost your immune system and give yourself a jolt of joy (see A Pause For Wild Swimming, p. 56).

- ✧ Take your most troubled thoughts, sad feelings or stuck decisions on a long walk, and they are almost sure to shift (see A Pause For Walking, p. 30).

- ✧ Run, skate or cycle on local trails (or see Find your flow, p. 100 for more ideas).

- ✧ Go to your local woodland and practise the Japanese art of Shinrin-yoku, or forest bathing (see Be mindful, p. 199).

- ✧ Move any other way you like outside. Dance freely, hula hoop or do yoga (see Embody, p. 119) in your garden, on the beach or in another outside space, perhaps, or climb a hill and hold your arms out to the wind to blow away the cobwebs in your brain.

Late afternoon: On your return, change and warm up if you need to, then rest a while in whatever way you need. Refresh your whole system with a short breathing practice (see Breathe, p. 191 for three ideas), then refresh your spirit with something light but engaging that appeals to you such as listening to music with attention, reading a short story, sketching or crafting, before making yourself a body-nourishing meal.

Evening: Prioritise what will help you have a good night's sleep, which is for many people the ultimate refreshment. Body brush again, then have a warm shower or bath. If you're bathing, a soak with Epsom salts is a great choice – they're a naturally occurring pure mineral compound of magnesium and sulphate that can help your body relax and cleanse. Then enjoy a warm, soothing caffeine-free drink. Allow yourself to turn out the light at a decent time.

Tips for a successful practice

- ✧ Spend a little time before this retreat day thinking about what 'refreshment' means to you, so you can pepper your day with activities that suit.
- ✧ To refresh your body from the inside out, today is a good day to be mindful of what and how you eat, and to drink oodles of water (see Retreat nourishment, p. 33).
- ✧ For an easy way to settle yourself after your outside activity, tune in to your body (see De-excite, p. 163).
- ✧ For sleep tips, see A Pause For Sleep (p. 137).

Reflect on your practice

Shortly after your day of refreshment, simply notice what has shifted. What feels different in your body and mind – your pace, your energy, your attitude? What cleansing rituals, and energising activities in nature, did you enjoy, and might do again?

Continue your practice

Bring refreshment into your daily life in whatever way works for you, from morning to night. Chop fresh ginger root, steep it in freshly boiled water, then strain it and store in the fridge. Each morning, sip some of it with hot water and lemon, or with room-temperature water and a splash of apple cider vinegar for a cleansing tonic. Bring body and tongue brushing into your daily routine too, and a body scrub into your weekly or monthly routine. Purify yourself with a cold shower whenever you need to wake up, and move outside in the elements each and every day. As many evenings as you can during a working week, make having a refreshing sleep your goal.

A PAUSE FOR WILD SWIMMING

Swimming outdoors in fresh or salt water such as rivers, lakes, lochs and the sea offers a direct, immersive connection to nature. It can be done in a multitude of peaceful or adventurous settings worldwide, from dedicated swimming ponds in local parks to quiet forest streams or rugged coastal waters, and it's a great alternative to swimming pools – especially if your local pool is chlorinated or users are susceptible to lane rage!

While a muscle-soothing swim in the warm Mediterranean sea can be a delightful tonic, swimming in cold water provides an extra boost to our physical and mental health. Cold-water immersion creates a mild stress response that narrows blood vessels, increases heart rate and adrenaline, and triggers the release of mood-boosting hormones, all of which can ease anxiety, support heart health and strengthen immunity.

The Wim Hof method takes this further, by combining cold exposure with specific breathing techniques (see A Pause For Our Breath as a Bridge, p. 192). Swimming in natural water is also a wonderful way to release negative energy and let go of things that no longer serve you, most especially if you put your head underneath. It's a regular go-to for me, and inspired my poem 'How To Give What You Don't Need To The Sea' (see p. 275).

Hosted retreats for refreshment

Adventure retreats: Hosted adventurous retreats of all kinds enable you to refresh yourself with movement in some of the world's most spectacular locations, from coastal swimming, surfing and stand-up paddleboarding breaks to hiking, biking and horse-riding escapes in the mountains. Many of these include daily Yoga classes to soothe tired muscles and ground you, while some offer access to spas so you can sweat out your toxins in steam rooms and saunas, or with hammam rituals, scrubs and wraps.

Detox retreats: To refresh yourself more intensely and for longer, a detox retreat intensifies our body's natural cleansing processes and gives us a chance to heal, rest and rebalance. Devised by doctors and nutritionists, the best detox retreats round the world range from gentle holistic cleanses, to educational gut health weekends, to intensive juice fasts. Whatever you choose, sessions of Yoga and Meditation, and activities such as treatments, nutritional consultations and optional enemas and colonics, help support your process.

Ayurveda retreats: A holistic health system devised by Indian sages over 5,000 years ago, Ayurveda is a Sanskrit word meaning the knowledge (*veda*) of life (*ayur*). It comes from the Veda, the ancient body of knowledge that is also the source of Yoga (see Embody, p. 119) and Vedic Meditation (see De-excite, p. 163). Ayurveda's focus is to keep us well by rebalancing our three bodily constitutions, called *doshas*, which are: Vata (air and ether, governing movement and the nervous system), Pitta (fire and water, metabolism and digestion) and Kapha (earth and water, strength and energy).

The most effective way to do this is to undertake a Panchakarma at an Ayurveda retreat. Literally meaning 'five therapies', this is a deeply cleansing programme of purifying treatments, nourishing meals and tonics, gentle movement and deep rest, all tailored to your specific *dosha* imbalance. The ideal length of time is three weeks or more for you to see the full effects, but there are much shorter retreats available, and therapists around the globe who offer consultations and some of the most soothing Ayurveda therapies as one-off treatments. For more, see Resources p. 261.

RETREAT FOR LONGER
DECLUTTER YOUR STUFF

I was once captivated by an elegant woman in a black dress whom I happened to meet on a slow boat along the Mekong River in Laos. She had been exploring for months, happily carrying only one soft bag, whereas I was carting about a heavy, unwieldy rucksack for a much shorter trip. We got on well, as the boat meandered along, and I wrote a poem about her later, which it felt fitting to keep short:

Filomena

She travels with just a cloth bag—
a chestnut-coloured tote—
so she can only pack small things:
her silver rings and antidotes.

Travelling light – in all senses of the word – has always appealed to me, and I've tried to learn over time, like Filomena, to leave things behind and trust that I will have all I need, at home as well as away. This is the essence of decluttering. If you have a lot of 'stuff' weighing you down, it might be time to try it.

First used as a verb in *Vogue* magazine in the 1950s, 'declutter' defines the simple, therapeutic process of removing unnecessary items from an untidy, cramped or overcrowded place in order to create an environment to live in that feels right for you. As minimalist living advocate Francine Jay so rightly puts it in her book, *The Joy of Less*: 'Your home is living space, not storage space'.

You don't have to be a minimalist to declutter, though. The key to your success is in your definition of 'unnecessary', which will probably vary greatly from your friend's or neighbour's. You don't have to get rid of most of your things, strip your house bare and paint your walls white to achieve a space in which you can thrive. I would have had a slightly larger tote bag than Filomena's, even in my ideal travelling scenario. Ask yourself, what do *you* need to live the life that *you* want?

Decluttering can feel difficult at times because it can feel emotional. As you go through your things, you can get caught in loops of distracting or painful memories, and it can be easy to sabotage yourself with unhelpful phrases, such as 'why did I buy this rubbish?' or 'how am I so disorganised?' There's a certain amount of fear too around being able to let things go. But as we sort through and reframe our stuff, we have the opportunity to sort through and reframe our thoughts.

Take time out to clear some clutter

I suggest three days for this retreat, but you could contract or expand the process, depending on whether you want to spend less or more time decluttering. Start small, choosing a carefully defined space that you can comfortably sort in a few days. Aim to finish with a sense of achievement that might encourage you to keep going another time. Choose a space you feel drawn to, and have the energy for. It could be your whole bedroom, or just your wardrobe. Your kitchen, or just your store cupboards. Your home office, or just your desk. Perhaps even a drawer of your desk! Each day, take regular breaks to move, rest and nourish yourself whenever you feel the need.

Suggested schedule

Day one: Sort and sift

Visualise your new space: On waking, think about the space you have picked to declutter, and ask yourself how you want that space to look afterwards. In your journal or on loose paper, jot down your intentions for the space so that you can come back to them later, including plans to move furniture around if you want to. Let yourself write freely. Do you want a colour co-ordinated capsule wardrobe in your bedroom, or space to sit and think in your sitting room? Do you want your desk to be facing a view and completely clear, or set up with practical things for work?

Sort and sift: After breakfast, dress in comfortable clothes you're happy to get dusty and dirty if need be. Take everything out of the space you have chosen to declutter and put it in another room. Don't pause. Work quickly. Have music on, a window open, a glass of water to hand – whatever works for you.

Pick each item up, one by one, and ask yourself three questions:

- Do I love this? Is this beautiful and/or of essential emotional value to me? If yes, put it on a 'love' pile.
- Do I need this? Is this truly useful and practical to me on a regular basis? Have I used it in the last three months? If yes, put it on a 'need' pile.
- Do I really want this? For everything else, it's usually a no. Have the courage to put it on a 'let go' pile. If you can't decide, put it on a 'don't know' pile for now.

Continue to sort through the things in your chosen space like this until you feel satisfied, taking breaks as you need, then give yourself time to relax and replenish yourself before sleep.

Day two: Rearrange and review

Clean and rearrange: If you want to spend more time decluttering, don't panic! Just carry on. Once you are ready, clean the space you have decluttered. Put your 'don't know' and 'let go' piles in a different place – you will deal with them later. Clean the items in your 'love' and 'need' piles, if necessary. Check your journal for notes on how you wanted this space to look and rearrange any large furniture accordingly. Have a window open to allow fresh air to circulate. Take things slowly. Enjoy the process.

Reinstall: Mindfully put the items you want to keep back into the space. Put your 'love' items on display or store them in a favourite box. Store your 'need' items tidily, taking a moment to ensure you have only kept what you really need (a spatula may be a vital item for your kitchen, but do you really need three of them? Keep the one you like best, and so on).

Review your 'don't know' pile: After a break, ideally outside in nature, sift through your 'don't know' pile again, using the same decluttering process as before. Put anything you remain unsure of away in a 'don't know' box or bag, and set a date in your calendar for three months' time to go through it again. If you haven't used or missed those items in that time, treat them as you would your 'let go' pile.

Continue your process until you run out of steam, then do something entirely different, away from your decluttered space, before sleep. Reassure yourself that you still have tomorrow to get things sorted.

Day three: Complete and celebrate

Deal with your 'let go' pile: Giving yourself this third day adds a sense of spaciousness to your self-devised declutter retreat. Finish up anything you left over from yesterday, then sort your 'let go' pile into bags to donate, recycle or sell responsibly.

If you feel energised, you could take some of these items out of the house straight away – to a local charity shop, for example. Put anything else you can't deal with today tidily out of sight – in your garage, shed, a cupboard, or under your bed. Set a date in your calendar when you can deal with them, but the sooner the better.

Conclude and celebrate: If you don't finish everything you want to, put a date in your diary for when you will do so. Then tidy things up, until you feel a sense of completion you are happy with for now. Congratulate yourself on the progress you have made with your new space. Celebrate by doing something that you love, alone or with others. Before sleep, treat yourself as if you, too, are decluttered, by bathing and putting on some fresh pyjamas!

Tips for a successful practice

- ✧ Consider scheduling your declutter for after you have been away from home for a few days or more. Being away from your space gives you a fresh perspective on it, as Leonardo Da Vinci observed (see p. 5). As soon as you walk through the door, it's easier to intuit what feels and looks right, and what doesn't. I find I often declutter spontaneously on return from a hosted retreat.

- ✧ Underestimate yourself and start small, so you feel a real sense of achievement at the end. Decluttering happens best in tiny steps.

- ✧ If you get stuck, do as Japanese Organising Consultant Marie Kondo would do, using her KonMari Method, and ask, 'does this bring me joy?' You'll be surprised how easily it helps you make your choice.

- ✧ If you continue to be tortured by doubt about a particular thing, ask yourself, will this help me live the remarkable life I want to live? Usually it's a resounding 'no!'

- ✧ For extra tips on help with your clothes, see A Pause For The Capsule Wardrobe opposite.

A PAUSE FOR THE CAPSULE WARDROBE

One reason we feel more relaxed on a holiday or at a hosted retreat is that we've pre-selected our clothes, so we don't have to think about what to wear and can focus instead on rest and renewal. At home, we regularly wear only a fraction of what we own, so why not recreate that ease by decluttering your wardrobe and making it more like a travelling bag?

A capsule wardrobe is a small, thoughtfully curated collection of clothing that can be mixed and matched to create a variety of outfits. The idea is to focus on quality over quantity, with versatile, timeless pieces that reflect your style and reduce the need for constant shopping. Creating your own capsule wardrobe is a brilliant way to reduce clutter, simplify getting dressed and free up your energy. It makes fashion more sustainable too.

If you are not going to focus on your wardrobe on your chosen declutter retreat, put a date in your diary for when you can. Then start with an audit – what clothes are working for you, what is not, and what is missing? You could choose one outfit you know you love for the key daily activities in your life, such as work, going out, relaxing and exercising, then build from there.

Keep pieces that feel fantastic and pair well with at least three other items you already own. Organise clothes by type for easy mix-and-matching. Store out-of-season clothes and donate, recycle or sell unwanted items.

When it comes to what clothes you feel are missing, be more considered about what you buy to minimise your choices, clutter and consumption. For every new piece added to your wardrobe, donate one, and reassess what you wear each season.

Consider following The Rule of Five campaign established by British fashion writer and activist Tiffanie Darke, who advises we buy just five new clothing items per year, excluding underwear, activewear and second-hand finds. 'This is a tangible way to help sustain the planet, whilst still enjoying the creativity and confidence of fashion,' says Tiffanie, who advises we make 60–80 per cent of our clothes functional, foundational pieces, and 20–40 per cent the colourful items that reflect our personality.

Reflect on your practice

After your declutter, consider how you feel about your newly decluttered space. Is there anything you'd still like to do to finish it? If you feel inspired, start a list of other spaces and rooms you would like to declutter.

Continue your practice

If you like decluttering, pick away at the items in your home, pile by pile, drawer by drawer, room by room, in any spare hours and days throughout the rest of your year. It's a ritual that I perform regularly, especially when I'm stressed. I find that, a little like weeding my garden, clearing my space of items I no longer need can help clear my mind and calm my anxieties.

Donate, recyle or sell items responsibly, and, going forward, be more considerate about what you buy. Reducing our consumption reduces our impact on the planet, as well as on the state of our homes and minds. Anytime you are stuck, just put things away for three months, then revisit them. You'll be surprised how much easier it is to let go of things you weren't sure about after a little time has passed.

Letting go of things we don't need on every level is what much of retreating is all about, and decluttering helps us reclaim space, time and energy for ourselves. To take this further, see A Pause For Letting Go, p. 130.

CONNECT

*'We have so little of each other, now. So far
from tribe and fire'*

Danusha Laméris, 'Small Kindnesses'

Who or what do you feel most connected to in your life today? If you feel lost, lonely or out of sorts, you may have become disconnected from what truly matters. Reconnecting can renew your sense of purpose and guide you towards what sustains you – within yourself, in nature and in relationships.

The word 'connect' comes from the Latin *connectere*, meaning 'to join together'. Connection is far more than a link; it's an invisible thread weaving through all our experiences, grounding us and helping us feel part of something larger.

We are more alike than different. World traditions, from Yoga and Buddhism to indigenous teachings, affirm our unity with each other and the planet. Our future and wellbeing also depend on us recognising our deep connection with nature.

How much time do you have to retreat?

- An hour – Journal (p. 69)
- A day – Garden (p. 74)
- Longer – Be kind (p. 82)

Whatever you choose, refer to the Retreat Toolkit (p. 15) to help you prepare for each retreat.

Start with a check-in

Write in your journal or think to yourself:

- *How loud is your inner voice, and what is it currently saying to you?*
- *When you see the word 'nature', what things come to mind?*
- *When was the last time you spoke to someone you don't know?*

RETREAT FOR AN HOUR
JOURNAL

I have kept a journal since I was eleven years old, to record, unload and explore all manner of things. I've always called it a diary, but I realise now that what I've been doing is journalling. While traditional diaries, commonplace books and daily logs mainly record external events, journalling is a deliberate practice of exploring and reflecting on one's thoughts, feelings and experiences, so that we can stay connected to ourselves.

Journalling has been practised in various forms for centuries. From Marcus Aurelius, whose private *Meditations* later shaped Stoic philosophy, to writers such as Sylvia Plath and Malala Yousafzai, who drew on their personal journals for powerful works that gave voice to inner struggle and resilience. It gained traction as a therapeutic tool in the 1960s, when American psychologist Dr Ira Progoff suggested his patients use a 'psychological notebook' to help explore their inner lives.

Today, journalling is used by people from all walks of life as a private tool for self-exploration. It is not the same as Morning Pages or free-flow writing to clear your mind (for this, see Clear your mind, p. 47).

Many of us write out of necessity, usually on a screen, in carefully thought-through emails or messages, designed to be read by others. But journalling is putting pen or pencil to paper in an honest conversation with just yourself. So that you can relax, get to know yourself better, and work out where you are now and what you might need, in your lifestyle, career or relationships.

You don't have to be 'good at writing' to journal – you just need to be able to write. The joy of it, and sometimes its challenge, is that it requires total honesty to work. It's not a post, caption or message you carefully curate for others to see. It's *your* space, to say what feels instinctive and true to you. It doesn't work for everyone, but if you find it works for you, this accessible practice can have multiple benefits.

Journalling can help you to:

- ✧ Tap into where you are at in your life, work or relationships, and watch your inner dialogue and the way you interact.
- ✧ Reveal patterns in your thinking and behaviour, as well as what you already know in your gut – your inner wisdom.
- ✧ Work through and reduce stress, self-sabotaging thoughts and negative thinking.
- ✧ Understand what truly matters to you – your core 'values' (see Re-imagine your life, p. 236) – and think creatively about any changes you want to make.
- ✧ Plan your time more effectively and solve problems more efficiently.

Take an hour to start journalling

Pick an hour when you know you will have some peace and privacy, and the energy to consciously engage with yourself. It could be when you first wake, or later in your day when you are outdoors in nature, or sitting quietly with a soothing drink.

Make sure you are somewhere alone, so you feel relaxed and less likely to censor your writing. Choose a favourite pen or pencil and a fresh notebook. If you're new to journalling, you could just use loose paper while you try it out.

Starting on a new page, write for your hour, trying out one of the techniques below to see what works for you. Keep going for your full hour, and you will begin to access what you might need today to take you into your tomorrow. When you have finished, pop your pages somewhere safely private, then move on with your day.

Journalling techniques to try

Write freely: I find free-flow writing works best for journalling, with no agenda. If you're stuck on what to write about at first, start by describing what you did yesterday, and how you felt about it. You could move on to what's going on in your home, at work, or in your relationships. What you feel sad or happy about at the moment. What you like and what you resist. As William Wordsworth put it in a letter he wrote to his wife, Mary: 'Fill your paper with the breathings of your heart.'

Journal prompts: There are some notebooks on the market with existing journal prompts in them, which can be useful if you want to be guided on how to check in with yourself, but that might also feel restrictive. I have developed my own journal prompts over time that help me focus when I write. Feel free to develop your own.

Some ideas for journal prompts include:

'My truths today': Write this phrase with a colon. Below it, write the first thing that comes to mind, then after a dash, try to free flow a little about that subject, then move on to the next 'truth'. Sometimes you'll only have a few, sometimes many. Each time you write a 'truth', try mapping out the thoughts, feelings and experiences that come to you quickly and easily. Afterwards pause, read it all back and see if anything else emerges before moving on to the next one.

It might prove fruitful to reflect on these truths and see what you can take forwards as lessons learned into the next prompt.

'Principles to live by until . . .': Try this prompt if you want to summarise with clarity certain promises you have made to yourself. Consider giving each principle a deadline, which could be as early as 'this evening', or as late as a few months away. It's best to keep it tight, and put in an actual date, to hold yourself to account.

'Relevant questions': Alternatively, write a list of questions relevant to you, to check in with yourself each day, making your own up to suit where you are at in your life. You might start with: What was I hard on myself about yesterday? Was I gentle enough with my family? What do I feel scared of today? Where in my body do I feel anxious? Where will I meditate this afternoon? What will make me happy this evening? And so on.

Tips for a successful practice

- Let yourself go and don't judge. This isn't a memoir, a social media post or an Instagram photo caption, so let everything out. Swear and shout if you need to, express all your angers, hungers and loves. Know, too, it's okay to waffle and repeat yourself – eventually you'll get into your own rhythm.

- Feel free to also doodle and sketch to express yourself alongside your words, if you're more of a visual person.

- If you need a kick start, consider simply making lists beginning with verbs, such as *I want* . . . , *I feel* . . . , *I need* . . . , I admire . . . , I relish . . . , and so on.

- If your head is full of clutter, consider 'offloading' first, then segue into journalling to process, organise and reflect (see Clear your mind, p. 47).

Reflect on your practice

Later that day or the next morning, ask yourself how you felt while you journalled, then re-read what you wrote. This can feel uncomfortable, but it can reveal useful truths and help you uncover what you want to do next. You might spot patterns of negative thinking or self-sabotage, or that you need to solve a practical issue at home or work. If you feel inspired, write another few pages.

Continue your practice

If you take to it, journalling can become a regular practice for you – daily, weekly or whenever you need it. If you carry on, it's best to use a dedicated notebook for it, different to the one you may be using to take you through this book (for more on retreat journalling, see p. 36).

You don't have to journal every day for it to serve you. Being on a hosted retreat or on holiday is a great opportunity for you to get into, or continue, a regular journalling practice, away from all distractions, and there's something delightful about taking a fresh new notebook with you when you go away.

Your regular journals can also become useful books packed full of creative ideas to draw on. Re-reading them can reveal all sorts of patterns that can be approached as clues to what we might do next, or do differently, or do more of. They can also be a gorgeous record of you and your life. Keep them somewhere safe and private. You could also pledge to declutter them after a set period of time (see Declutter your stuff, p. 58).

RETREAT FOR A DAY

GARDEN

I am in the garden, hands in the soil, pulling out weeds with relish from my favourite flower bed. As I scrape, prune and deadhead methodically, the sun on my face, a breeze on my skin, I zone out, and by the time I have finished, the persistent thoughts and small anxieties I came into the garden with have disappeared, leaving me unruffled for the rest of my afternoon. Such is the rejuvenating power of gardening, for which I – alongside so many others – found a passion during the global Covid-19 pandemic.

Garden designer and retreat leader Emma Clark reflects on this idea: 'When we design, prune, weed, deadhead, feed, plant and grow stuff in our gardens, we are nourishing the "good wolf" of our natures – our patience, kindness, courage, etc – over the "bad wolf" – our anger, jealousy, greed, etc.' You don't have to set the intention to let go of the 'bad wolf' feelings – you'll usually find they naturally work their way out of you as you garden.

It doesn't matter if you don't have your own garden, or the use of an outside space. You could tend to a friend's garden, start with a window box, trough or hanging basket, grow a small collection of plants in pots indoors, or on a balcony, deck or terrace. The key thing is to do it, because, as retreat leader, activist and former Jain monk Satish Kumar advises, 'gardening is essentially activism – a way of saving and changing ourselves.'

Whatever thoughts and emotions we may take with us to our tasks, we usually emerge feeling purged, more positive and better able to tackle the things ahead of us in our lives. Gardening is especially forgiving too – we can experiment, mess things up and still go on to witness gorgeous plants bloom with relatively little effort, giving us regular doses of mood-boosting joy.

Gardening:

- Helps us release our stress, calm our anxieties and ease our sadness.
- Boosts our confidence and gives us a sense of purpose and hope.
- Gives us a gentle or vigorous physical workout, and enables us to grow our own healthy things to drink and eat.
- Provides a canvas for our creativity, on which we can unleash our own designs for colour and form.
- Helps us connect with nature, which increases our respect for it and helps us take care of it better.

Take a day to get closer to nature

Choose how you will garden in advance, being mindful of what season you are in.

Take time to tap into what you really want to do, leaving any 'shoulds' aside. If your schedule allows, you could turn your garden planning time into a mini-retreat in and of itself. See ways to garden (below) and what to grow (p. 76) for ideas, and for Resources, see p. 261.

To add variety to your retreat day, select a way to create in nature too (see p. 77). A gardening retreat is a particularly easy one to share with children, a friend or a family member, if you so choose, so plan ahead accordingly (see Who to retreat with, p. 17). In case of bad weather, stay flexible with the retreat day you choose.

Ways to garden

If you are new to gardening or have limited outside space: Start small. Create a few pots, a hanging basket, a trough or a window box. Plant a few seasonal things from seed, or, for quicker results, buy starter plants.

If you have no outside space: Ask a friend or family member if you can garden in theirs, or consider an indoor planting project, such as a miniature zen garden made of stones and succulents, or a set of house plants.

If you're already a gardener: Will you carry on working on something you've started, prune or deadhead, or perhaps make a vegetable bed from scratch if you mainly grow flowers? Do you have a greenhouse you could use, to fast track something you haven't grown before?

Relish weeding: You could devote a whole morning to a satisfying spot of weeding. If your garden is neglected, there will be something supremely satisfying about spending your retreat day clearing a dedicated area of it.

What to grow

Flowers: Choose those you love to look at that suit the soil and climate of where you live. Try geraniums or dahlias for easy cheerfulness, irises and tulips for elegance, and roses for fragrance and beauty. Sowing a selection of wildflower seeds, in a trough or a bed you see often, creates unexpected joy as you watch the different flowers come up throughout the season. Try growing plants around rocks – daisies thrive like this if you tuck sprigs into little pockets of earth between stones or pavers.

A herb garden: Indoors in pots or outside in a rock garden, plant lemon balm, lemongrass or mint for herbal teas; rosemary, thyme or sage for herb-infused oils, salts or vinegars; and parsley, basil, chives or oregano for cooking.

Healthy plants: For outside, pick those with strong, relaxing fragrances, such as jasmine, gardenia and lavender, to ease stress and anxiety. Inside, unfussy, durable varieties of house plants with air-purifying qualities include snake plants and red-edged dracaena.

Things to eat: Try easy-to-grow prolific vegetables, such as carrots or courgettes, fruits such as strawberries or blueberries, or edible flowers such as nasturtiums, pansies and chive blossoms for pretty additions to dishes and drinks.

Don't forget weeds: Many plants we think of as 'weeds' provide colour and beauty with little need for care, and pollinators such as bees love them. Let dandelions, buddleia and clover run wild, along with forget-me-nots, nettles and cow parsley.

Ways to create in nature

Gardening is a creative act, but you could also try other creative pursuits during your retreat day to help you slow down, relax and engage with the natural world. Ideas include:

Nature crafting: Paint plant pots, press flowers to use as decorations in cards, or practise leaf art, by making pictures from garden leaves, clovers and ferns. If you have children, they will especially enjoy these tasks. You could also start bigger tasks – paint faded or mismatched garden furniture in a colour you love, for example, to co-ordinate and refresh your outside space, starting with just one piece on your retreat day.

Nature writing: Take a notebook to your garden or chosen green space and pick one small detail that draws you in: the texture of bark on a tree trunk, the colour of a group of wild flowers, or the movement of grasses in the wind, for example.

Spend time observing with each of your five senses, then write down your observations in fragments or as phrases, questions or written sketches. A list poem works well as a response: use repeated prompts, changing the last word each time, such as: *'Holding the soil, I sense . . .'* and *'Holding the soil, I see . . .'* and so on. Later, you might shape your notes into a short reflection, or keep them as simple records of attention.

Nature photography: Head outside with a camera (see tips for staying offline on p. 38 for what kind of camera to choose). Let something catch your eye – a patch of apple-green moss, a clutch of butter-yellow primroses, a huge pile of dried golden leaves, an intricate spider's web. To begin, choose one subject and try capturing it from different angles or in different lights, focusing more on observation than perfection. Afterwards, you might keep the images as quiet reminders, print them, share them, or decide to build a small series around a theme or place.

Suggested schedule

On waking: There is something very special about the early morning air. Open your window, or if you have a garden or outdoor space, go straight out into it, and simply breathe. Make a hot drink with a fresh plant such as mint. Stretch or do any regular practice you may have, outside in your garden if you can.

Morning: After breakfast, take a moment to consider what you're bringing into your day. Do you feel grumpy, angry, frustrated or tired? Is there something on your mind that you would like to let go of? Jot it down, or simply think it. Then get straight to your choice of gardening activity, breaking whenever you need to rest.

Afternoon: After lunch, carry on with your gardening if you are in the zone and don't want to stop. Or change the pace of your day to create in nature (see p. 77). How long you stay out may be weather or season dependent, but it can be delightful and soothing to stay outdoors until last light.

Evening: Consider what you took into your gardening day this morning, and how you now feel, and what you are thinking about, at the end of it. Has it changed?

Make a list of practical things you might want to do another time, so you can lay them to rest in your mind. Allow yourself time to ease out your weary muscles, perhaps in a bath or with some stretches. Before you turn out the light, ask yourself what delighted you today. Was it a feeling, a colour, a shape, some small achievement? Make a mental note to bring more of that into your life from now on.

Tips for a successful practice

- Checking the information on seed packets will quickly help you decide what you can plant now, how fast things will grow and how much space they will take up.

- Whatever your choice of tasks, let go of all perfectionism. The key thing is to participate in nature and witness what emerges.

- Bring a sense of calm and kindness to your day. I like writer Elizabeth von Arnim's description of gardening as solace in her 1899 book *The Solitary Summer:* 'Of what use is it to fight for things and make a noise? Nature is so clear in her teaching that he who has lived with her for any time can be in little doubt as to the "better way".'

- Bring a sense of wonder to what you see, and take your time to notice it. As activist Satish Kumar affirms: 'Nature is the star designer.' Describing the broad bean, for example, he says: 'Their cases are so beautifully prepped to protect the soft beds inside, where the beans rest as if in a cradle, covered by a tiny duvet, with a clever tail to hold everything together. This is not something tech could design!'

Reflect on your practice

The next day, consider your thoughts and feelings. Do you feel better in any way? Are you thinking differently about a situation or a person in your life? Did you leave anything that was agitating you behind in your garden or your green space of choice? What did you enjoy about creating in nature, if you did this? Jot down anything significant.

Continue your practice

If you take to gardening, keep going! Garden in your own space, join an allotment or a community gardening group. Bring the outside in by using the flowers, herbs and edible plants you've started to grow, or start a nature sketchbook that captures what you see and do in the garden and beyond. Nature crafting, writing and photography can be a real tonic throughout life. Take into nature all your agitations and angst and emerge released and relaxed, ready to take on your world again. Moving in nature is also a key part of this (see Refresh yourself, p. 51).

Hosted gardening retreats

Hosted gardening retreats come in a variety of forms, from immersive stays that combine hands-on workshops with seasonal cooking and a break from digital life to peaceful getaways where guests can volunteer to tend vegetable patches and flower borders, reconnecting with nature through mindful work in return for delicious food from the land and accommodation. Some retreats focus on practical skills, including garden design and flower arranging, while others blend creative pursuits, such as learning to paint flowers or exploring the history and symbolism of plants like the tulip.

RETREAT FOR LONGER

BE KIND

I have been saved by unexpected acts of kindness from strangers on many occasions. As a teenager, for example, when I received a thoughtful, hand-written reply to a letter I had addressed 'to anyone who will listen' and buried in the snow near my home. It was signed 'your fairy prince', and, to this day, I have no idea who sent it. Or, after a particularly hard day in my twenties, finding a bunch of flowers on my moped with a note: 'I felt like doing something silly and you're the victim.' Scared, lonely and unable to find a hotel room one night on my travels in India, in my thirties, a couple opened their doors to me and took me in.

Being kind is an easy way to connect with other people and boost our own wellbeing. It's a win-win. You might feel lonely, awkward or anxious in a situation, but if you perform a small act of kindness, you feel instantly more comfortable and connected to its recipient. You realise that the other person is just like you – even though they may be hidden behind a social mask you can't quite make out.

Being kind is also a way to embrace Freudenfreude, the experience of feeling joy or happiness for someone else's success or good fortune. Intentionally adopting this way of thinking helps us choose a different path to comparison and competition with others, and strengthens our friendships and wider community.

Sometimes, a simple act of care can become a lifeline for people who are struggling internally in ways we might not be able to see. We take for granted that other people are 'okay', where we might think we are not, but this is usually not the case. Everyone is buried in their own concerns, and in our world of tech, it's not so easy to lift up our heads and 'see' others. Doing so helps us come out of ourselves too.

Kindness is a thread that binds humanity, especially when there is seemingly conflict and intolerance all around us. As American poet and journalist Ella Wheeler Wilcox says in her 1906 poem:

The World's Need

So many gods, so many creeds,
So many paths that wind and wind,
While just the art of being kind
Is all the sad world needs.

Being kind:

- Connects us to those around us and helps us feel part of a better world.

- Takes us out of our own problems and into our hearts, reducing stress and opening us up.

- Supports healing and helps us find compassion for others and ourselves.

- Acts as an antidote to aggression and cruelty, spreading more kindness.

- Gives us and others real joy, and can be a great motivator.

Take time out to follow a schedule of kindness

Take three clear days off to follow a schedule of kindness, or longer if you choose. Ahead of time choose who to be kind to, and the ways you will be kind (see next page). Make sure the cadence of your retreat gives you variety and enough time to process how your behaviour is affecting you for the better, as well as to rest and replenish in between your kind acts.

Who to be kind to

During each day, plan to be kind to four people:

- Someone you know and like, such as a friend, family member or colleague – this could be someone in your daily life, or someone you don't see very often or who lives far away.
- A stranger.
- Someone who triggers you – this could be someone you know, have known in the past whose impact stays with you, or someone in the public eye.
- Yourself, because being kind to others starts by being kind to yourself (see Treat yourself, p. 126).

Ways to be kind

Treat your treasured people well: Often we can be the meanest to those closest to us, because we feel emotionally safe with them and trust that they will stick by us however we behave. But they deserve, and need, our kindness too. Listen to your friends and loved ones with sincere interest, and expect to make plans through compromise rather than trying to get your own way or always giving into theirs. Meet them as they are, rather than trying to find things about them you feel they should change, correct or improve. Most of all, if you don't live with them, meet them in person, as regularly as you can.

Remember those in your past who served you well: To honour someone you are no longer in touch with, you might simply include them in a note in your gratitude journal. But if you still have their address, why not reach out and surprise them with a friendly note? You never know where they are at in their lives – a friendly voice, even from the distant past, might be exactly what they need at a particular time.

Talk to strangers: Communicating with people who we do not know can be a way to practise kindness that can boost us in return. Educator and author Kio Stark, in her book *When Strangers Meet,* found that people are happier when they allow themselves to engage and talk with the strangers they meet throughout their day, even when they think they'll loathe it.

Even brief exchanges, such as saying thank you when receiving a coffee, can foster a sense of connection and wellbeing for both parties. It can also be easier to open up about difficult things to a stranger than a friend, as they give us space without entanglement, helping us share freely without burdening our closest bonds.

Perform unexpected acts of kindness: This is one of the most fun ways to be kind. Coined by writer Anne Herbert in 1980s California as a counter to random violence, her call to 'practise random kindness and senseless acts of beauty' invites us to meet the world with compassion through thoughtful, unreturned gestures. While the idea evokes anonymous gestures towards strangers, its spirit lies in doing something thoughtful without expecting anything in return – for family, friends or colleagues too. See box below for ideas.

IDEAS FOR UNEXPECTED ACTS OF KINDNESS

FOR THOSE YOU KNOW:

- Set the table for your family and grace it with a vase of fresh flowers.

- Cook a meal for a busy parent.

- Offer to wash someone's car or mow someone's lawn.

- Shop or carry bags for someone who's struggling, or bring a neighbour's bin in from the street.

- Lend a book or share a piece of music you love with someone who might enjoy it, with a note saying why it mattered to you.

- Message a friend about a favourite memory you share with them, just to say you were thinking of them.

- Take time to hand-write cards and letters and put them in the post, to mark important events or show your support for someone.

- Sit with, listen or read to someone you know who needs company.

- Make supportive voice or video notes for loved ones on the day you feel inspired to do so, to send to them later.

- Leave a small gift for someone when they least expect it, for no particular reason.

FOR THOSE YOU DON'T KNOW:

- Offer a gesture or question of concern to someone you see is clearly upset, rather than walking by.

- Voice a compliment to a stranger that you might usually withhold through shyness – 'that's a beautiful dress', say, or, 'I really appreciate your smile'.

- Pay for the coffee or cake of the person behind you in line, just to brighten their day or help them out.

- Leave a kind, anonymous note in a public place – such as in a book in a bookshop or library or on a park bench – for someone to find when they might need it most.

- Let someone go ahead of you in a queue if they seem rushed or frazzled.

- Place a bunch of herbs or garden flowers in a jar on a bench or doorstep with a note that says 'Take me'.

- Offer to carry heavy shopping at the supermarket, or lift heavy bags from an airport carousel or train rack.

- Share food and drink on a journey, a walk or on a mountaintop.

- Go and thank your local refuse collectors or road sweepers for the job they do.

- Pick up litter wherever you find it for the benefit of everyone.

- Join your local repair café to help people save money, reduce waste, share skills and build community.

Suggested schedule

On waking each day: You could start with a Loving Kindness Meditation (see p. 91). Then do something that feels nurturing and kind to yourself. Stay in bed longer than you usually do.

Allow yourself a hot chocolate, instead of a herbal tea, if you never do so and fancy one. Have a bath rather than your usual workout. Get out in the fresh air to walk and leave the washing-up behind. You'll know what feels kind to you. Usually it's taking away a lot of the 'shoulds' we carry around in life, especially when it comes to our domestic sphere.

Before sleep each day: Choose something each evening that supports you kindly into sleep. Read a poem that promotes gentleness or patience. Nurture yourself with a warm bath or shower and a hot drink. If you have missed your Loving Kindness Meditation in the morning, now is a good time. Gift yourself the chance of a good night's sleep and allow yourself to wake naturally tomorrow.

Day one: Surprise and share

Morning: Go out and perform your first unexpected act of kindness for a stranger. Surprise yourself. You don't even need to plan it. Just take yourself on a local outing and have the intention of doing something spontaneous and kind. Be alert and you'll find your moment.

Afternoon: Is there someone who has been triggering you? Try writing a letter to them, not to post, but just to get it off your chest. Start by telling them how you are feeling, then find something in the situation that inspires your compassion, and write about that. See where the process leads you. Perhaps it will even inspire you to forgive. Do you need to reach out to them in person, or can you let the matter rest now? If you want to, use your journal to work things through.

Evening: You could make your first night entertaining for yourself. Go out alone, or with a significant other, or with a good friend you have missed seeing for a while. Share a film, live theatre, music gig or comedy show.

Day two: Suggest and socialise

Morning: Suggest a walk followed by brunch or lunch to a close friend or family member. Perhaps someone you feel has been asking for your time and attention recently, which you haven't been able to give. Go with the intention of listening to them. Try to avoid jumping in with your own stories and advice, or steering the conversation away from what they want to talk about.

Afternoon: Perform your second unexpected act of kindness for a stranger – plan this one ahead of time, so you know what you will do. Perhaps set the intention that, while out, you will talk in some small way to a stranger, no matter for how short a time. If you develop a conversation, resist asking them about their back story (see Tips, p. 91).

Evening: You could make the middle night of your retreat sociable if you choose. Start early, so you still have the chance of a good night's sleep afterwards. Have friends, family or colleagues over for a meal to connect. Or host a board games night, karaoke session or music jam – whatever inspires you and suits the group you want to see. Ask someone to bring a new friend along who you don't know, and challenge yourself to simply meet them in the moment, and not to ask them what they 'do'.

Day three: Provide and process

Morning: Sit down and write a thoughtful card or letter to a friend, family member or colleague who means something to you. Surprise them. Pop it in the post.

Afternoon: Is there someone you know who might appreciate some help that you never seem to find the time to give? A family member who is struggling? An older person who might want to be read to or just sat with? A busy parent who might need help cleaning their house or cooking their family a meal? Give them a few hours of your time and attention today.

Evening: Take the last evening to yourself to rest and process. Journal about your experiences. Which of the activities have you enjoyed the most? What has surprised you the most? Who did you pick for your Loving Kindness Meditations? Why do you think that was? Has practising kindness helped ease any anger or frustration you might feel? What else has triggered or supported you? How has being kind made you feel? Will you carry on with your random acts of kindness?

A PAUSE FOR BEFRIENDING

One of the most startling sentences I heard, just after the Covid-19 pandemic and the global lockdowns, was in a talk by Buddhist Meditation teacher Ramiro Ortega. 'Imagine the world as a hospital, with all the unkind people in the world the ones who are ill. We need to treat them with compassion,' he said. Without kindness, mindfulness is 'just focus', so we need to see mindfulness as a kind of 'befriending'.

Buddhist teacher Christina Feldman describes 'befriending' not as a practice to switch on and off, but as an ongoing attitude of kindness and compassion towards ourselves, strangers and those we dislike. True befriending, she notes, arises when we care without needing to judge, fix or control, pausing instead to meet moments of judgement or impatience with patience and acceptance.

The Buddhist practice of Metta, or *Loving Kindness Meditation*, is a compelling way to increase this ability to befriend and practise kindness, compassion, acceptance and understanding. You don't have to be a Buddhist to do this, just possess a willing heart. For more on Buddhism, see p. 216.

HOW TO DO A LOVING KINDNESS MEDITATION

- Find a quiet place to sit comfortably and close your eyes. Begin by silently repeating these kind phrases towards yourself: 'May I be happy, may I be healthy, may I be safe, may I live with ease.'

- After a few minutes, bring someone you love to mind and repeat the same phrases for them: 'May you be happy', and so on.

- Then, do the same for someone you feel neutral about, someone you find difficult (such as someone who has triggered you in your life, recently or in the past, or someone who is in the public eye), and, finally, for all beings.

- Breathe naturally throughout. When you are ready, gently open your eyes.

Tips for a successful practice

- Remember you are on retreat, so protect your time and energy. Don't overschedule yourself, and ensure that anything you arrange feels uplifting rather than tiresome. If cooking drains or bores you, for example, but you want people over, have drinks instead, and serve easy-to-prepare finger food. The focus is on communicating and practising kindness, not creating more work for yourself.

- Take your time and slow down. Being kind is connected to being mindful of the things and people around you (see Be mindful, p. 199). Honour how introverted or extroverted you are in this process. Arrange meetings if you thrive on company, or just perform kind activities if you'd prefer your own company. Keep electronic devices off if you can.

- When meeting someone new, set aside your back story – it makes for kinder, more honest conversations. Skip 'what do you do?' and ask instead, 'what's coming up for you this weekend?' or simply, 'what's happening?'

- Know that you don't have to be a particular kind of person to be kind. I love the poet Emily Dickinson's take on it, in her 1877 poem:

They might not need me—yet they might—
I'll let my Heart be just in sight—
A smile so small as mine might be
Precisely their necessity.

- Expect nothing in return when you give by being kind. Just know that kindness has a way of circling back – if not from the recipient, then from life in other ways. This can feel hard if your efforts go unnoticed, so be kind to yourself and trust that kindness will still spread.

Reflect on your practice

After your retreat, ask yourself how being kind has made you feel. Are there any activities or tricks you'd like to repeat and bring into your daily life? Choose something easy to pledge to repeat regularly, to help take a spark of kindness forwards – such as smiling at a stranger who helps you in some way – each and every day.

Continue your practice

Carry on being kind on a daily basis. Draw on the activities that have resonated with you. You could look for regular volunteering opportunities or community work to take you out of yourself. Listen to podcasts or guided meditations that promote patience, listening and kindness. Or go further and do something more dramatically kind, such as mentoring a teenager who needs guidance, or tutoring someone who needs it for free.

Kindness on hosted retreats

Going on a hosted retreat can be a good environment in which to connect with new people and enjoy the kindness of strangers. Some of the most powerful retreat experiences can be found in a group where no one knows each other. When you connect deeply with people you may never meet again, you can truly open up and share difficult things more easily than you might be able to with those familiar to you.

Retreating is also a kind act towards yourself, which is why you might struggle to make going on one a priority. I know many busy working parents, for example, who see a retreat as a one-off 'treat' that misplaced guilt often prevents them from 'indulging' in. Yet if you turn that around, and retreat regularly, you'll find that you have more calm and energy for the very dependants you feel you 'should' be looking after instead of retreating.

If you take to the morning Loving Kindness Meditation, you could explore this further by going on a Buddhist retreat (see A Pause for Buddhism, p. 216). If you've found it difficult to be kind to your partner, consider a Couples Retreat for counselling. Or if you feel disconnected from them, a well-sourced Tantra Retreat, which encourages being present and deep listening with each other, could be just the ticket.

CREATE

'In art as in love, instinct is enough'
Anatole France, *The Garden of Epicurus*

How does creativity show up in your life? The word 'create' comes from the Latin *creare*, meaning 'to make, bring forth, produce'. Creativity isn't just found on a canvas or stage; it can be present in your daily life – from what we cook or wear to the way we solve a problem or plan a party.

Nurturing our imagination and inventiveness helps us to shape the life we want and discover new ways of seeing and doing. To do so we need to be brave. To smother the voices that doubt our creations – from teachers or parents who questioned our art as children to our critical inner voices today.

When we find our courage, we can use creativity to connect with where we are in life, to find our flow and to flourish. We can become artists on our own terms.

How much time do you have to retreat?

- ✧ An hour – Make a mark (p. 97)
- ✧ A day – Find your flow (p. 100)
- ✧ Longer – Be an artist (p. 108)

Whatever you choose, refer to the Retreat Toolkit (p. 15) to help you prepare for each retreat.

Start with a check-in

Write in your journal or think to yourself:

- ✧ *When faced with a blank piece of paper, I usually . . .*
- ✧ *Activities I loved most when I was a child included . . .*
- ✧ *A creative activity I have always longed to try but never dared to is . . .*

RETREAT FOR AN HOUR
MAKE A MARK

When was the last time you reached for a pencil and drew something? Having the courage to freely express yourself on a blank piece of paper can be therapeutic, and you don't have to be 'arty' or know how to draw to do it. This is the principle behind Art Therapy, a refreshingly different, in-the-moment practice that helps us relax, observe ourselves without judgement and reconnect with what's important in our lives.

People have drawn on the healing power of art since ancient times, but the term Art Therapy was first coined in the 1940s by British artist Adrian Hill. In his book *Art Versus Illness*, he describes how making art during his tuberculosis treatment in a sanatorium aided his recovery, and how he encouraged other patients to do the same.

I first experienced the practice on a retreat in Crete with art therapist Penelope Orfanoudaki, who explains: 'Art Therapy uses "mark making" to help you connect with yourself and whatever is going on in your world at the moment. You don't have to be traumatised to do it, just dealing with the stresses of daily life.'

Art therapy can help you:

- Work through inner tensions.
- Regulate your emotions.
- Calm the nervous system.
- Grow in self-confidence.
- Become more self-aware.

Take an hour to make art without judgement

Gather a plain, white piece of paper (A4 is a good size), a pencil and colours of your choice. This could simply be coloured pencils or pens, or crayons, acrylic paint, pastels or watercolours if you have them. Then choose one of these three techniques, which I learned from Penelope:

- On a white piece of paper, make a circle. Imagine this circle as part of an image. Complete the image.

Or

- On a white piece of paper, draw a line. Imagine this line as a connector or separator in an image. Complete the image.

Or

- On a white piece of paper, draw three dots. Connect these dots in any way you want to complete the image.

Start immediately, without any plan. As you draw, you get to decide how big your circle is, how long your lines are, whether they are curly or straight, and where you should place them on the paper. Colour and embellish your image in the time you have, using any mix of materials you choose.

Observe your image. What do you see? How does it make you feel? Why do you think you chose that particular colour, or made that particular shape? Write down any thoughts in your journal or on loose paper. Give your artwork a title, set it aside and get on with your day.

Tips for a successful practice

- Don't judge yourself – there is no right or wrong. Allow yourself to be playful rather than overthinking things.

- ✧ Feel free to experiment with different shades and forms to express how you feel. As artist Georgia O'Keeffe says: 'I found I could say things with colour and shapes that I couldn't say any other way – things I had no words for.'

- ✧ If you feel comfortable, ask a friend or partner you trust to make their own creation alongside you, then discuss them afterwards together, with kindness and without judgement. Making art in the company of others can be fun and helps you feel a sense of belonging.

Reflect on your practice

Allow your creation to percolate in your mind during the course of your day. If you like, carry the title you gave your work with you too. That evening, ask yourself, has it provided any insights? What might your creation, or your feelings about it, say about how you are and any changes you might need to make? If you feel like it, discuss it with someone you trust.

Continue your practice

You can use the same practice to check in with yourself whenever you want, spending longer or shorter on your piece of art as you need. It will never be the same experience. To take things further and reap the benefits of being able to share insights as part of a supportive group, book a session with an art therapist, join an Art Therapy workshop in person or online, or attend an Art Therapy retreat for a fully immersive experience (see Resources, p. 261).

RETREAT FOR A DAY
FIND YOUR FLOW

You know that feeling where you are so engaged with an activity that you have lost track of time and nothing else matters? This is what psychologist Mihaly Csikszentmihalyi calls the 'flow state', an intense experience of immersion and joy, in which we lose our self-consciousness and access our deepest creativity.

Writers call it 'the muse'; drummers 'finding the pulse'; jazz musicians 'being in the pocket'. Bloomsbury artist Vanessa Bell sums it up well when she says: 'It is indeed so exciting and so absorbing, this painter's world of form and colour, that once you are at its mercy you are in grave danger of forgetting all other aspects of the material world.'

Flow requires passion and focus, and happens when there's just enough challenge to focus your attention, but not so much that it feels overwhelming. 'If it's too hard, you'll feel anxious; if it's too easy, it becomes boring,' explains trauma therapist Josh Dickson, who runs surf-therapy retreats to help others through trauma using flow. 'When the difficulty is just enough to stretch us, and we're focused and ready, flow becomes possible.'

When you find your flow:

- ✧ You are entirely absorbed in what you're doing, and your actions feel effortless and purposeful.

- ✧ Time slips away, self-consciousness fades and worries or tensions dissolve.

- ✧ You emerge elated yet grounded, feeling fulfilled by the experience.

- ✧ Creative ideas bubble up, leaving you energised to bring them to life.

✧ You feel more connected – to yourself, to others and to the wider thread of your life.

Over the course of my life I have found my flow through ballet, swimming, writing and Yoga. Josh, meanwhile, has found his through surfing and making music, and friends I know have found theirs through walking, climbing, singing and working with clay. What about you? If you're feeling a little stuck in life, now's the time to find out.

Take a day to access your flow state

Pick one, two or three activities with which to populate this retreat day, so you can experiment with finding flow. You will ideally already love the activities you choose, or have a deep curiosity about them. Choose ones that stretch your ability and give you in-the-moment feedback, so you know that what you are doing is working for you. For ideas for flow activities, see below.

You should ideally be able to do your flow-inducing activities in your chosen retreat space, or be able to reach them easily without having far to travel. Some could involve attending a lesson or a workshop, or playing a team game – in which case, build your schedule around that. Feel free to share an activity with a friend or family member but keep at least one of them to do alone. During each activity, you'll know whether you've found your flow and when you have had enough.

Ideas for flow activities

PHYSICAL PURSUITS
Movement on land: Walk, hike or run through forests, hills or coastal paths, or explore urban routes on foot, by skateboard, skates or bike – even pushing into Parkour if you're experienced. Ride road or mountain bikes across countryside or forest tracks, shifting pace and terrain for variety.

Adventure in nature: Swim or paddle board in pools, rivers, lakes or the sea, or try bodyboarding and surfing in the ocean, building confidence wave by wave. Climb boulders or scramble up rocks. In winter, take on skiing, snowboarding, ice skating or Nordic walking for fresh challenge.

Sports: Practise games such as tennis or badminton with serves, volleys, rallies or matches, or boost energy and focus with team sports like football and basketball. Mix solo drills with full games to balance precision and teamwork.

Dancing: Put on music you love and dance freely. If you're used to dance and structured moves, loosen them. If freeform is your comfort zone, challenge yourself with a new rhythm or style. Create your own silent disco in your garden or on the beach. Attend an ecstatic dance class (see Embody, p. 119).

Hula-hooping: Spin a hoop and play with rhythm and direction. If you're new to this, explore keeping it going for longer. If you're experienced, try new tricks or change your pace. Seek out a local session and try it alongside others.

Sequencing Yoga styles: Choose a steady style like Vinyasa, Ashtanga or Jivamukti. If you're a beginner or quite new to Yoga, seek out an extended in-person class, to learn and flow alongside others with the motivation of a teacher. If practised, stretch into a longer flow.

Qigong and Tai Chi: Move slowly and mindfully through flowing sequences that coordinate breath and gentle movement (see Embody, p. 119).

CREATIVE AND INTELLECTUAL PURSUITS
Collaging and crafting: Cut, arrange and layer images, patterns, textures or textiles. Experiment freely or build skills through simple stitches or more challenging patterns.

Drawing and painting: Work small-scale to practise precision, repetition and focus, or shift to large-scale, using big surfaces, full-body movement and bold gestures to energise your process.

Cooking and gardening: Immerse yourself in preparing a new recipe, or weed furiously, building up an energy (see Garden, p. 74).

Writing: Set a timer and write without editing. Engage in journalling, storytelling, rhythmic poetry or freewriting. Keep your pen or keys moving. If you're practised in one type of writing, try a new style or topic.

Reading: Whether it's something challenging or not, fiction or non-fiction, the key is to find a book that will immerse you entirely.

Making music: Compose your own piece, or pick up an instrument you know or one you've set aside for too long. Play patterns, improvise or learn something new. Drumming is especially good for getting you into a flow state. Play rhythms solo or in a group – find a workshop near you. If you know the basics, add layers or complexity. Sing and chant (see A Pause For Sound, p. 104).

Suggested schedule

Whatever you choose, keep your schedule really flexible, so that, after each activity, you can do something spontaneous as your mood suggests. You won't know until you're in that moment what this will be and what the rest of your day requires. You might want to journal, move your body, take a walk, or plan something new and exciting! Make sure you nourish and hydrate yourself throughout your day.

Morning: This could be an energising activity, done soon after waking.

Afternoon/Daytime: This could be a more substantial activity, perhaps one that takes you away from your retreat space and outside into nature, or taking part in a class.

Evening: This could be a gentler, more relaxing or creative activity, or an evening class or session. Give yourself a soft landing and time to relax before bed.

A PAUSE FOR SOUND

When you chant, sing or hum, the vibrations created in your throat and chest stimulate the vagus nerve, a key part of our relaxation system. This is the body's longest cranial nerve and connects our body to our brain, running via the neck to our chest and abdomen. Stimulating it helps activate your body's relaxation response, slowing your heart rate, reducing stress and making you feel more balanced and at ease.

This is why chanting or singing can be so relaxing and uplifting, alone or in a group, and can help you enter a flowing, creative and meditative state. Pick your favourite piece and use your voice to build sound alone or with others through repetition or improvisation. Sing familiar songs, or choose a favourite and create harmonies around it, a capella style. Try following chants from diverse traditions, such as the call-and-response singing of Kirtan in Yoga, or the rhythmic chanting of Pali verses in Theravāda Buddhism.

As many of us will know, you can also find flow by *listening* to sound, whether that's classical music or reggae, nature sounds or Gregorian chant. The rhythm and repetition help your mind focus, quieten distractions and guide you into a relaxed, absorbed state, where you lose track of time and feel fully present.

This is why a session of Sound Healing is so powerful – the therapist uses vibration and resonance, from instruments or voice, to calm the nervous system, release tension and restore a sense of balance. You might also experiment with music tuned to 432 Hz, which some listeners find more harmonious than the standard 440 Hz pitch. Some of Verdi's music was performed at 432 Hz, for instance.

Making and listening to sound is also a form of embodiment, because it deepens your awareness of how your body reacts to sensory input and fosters a direct, felt connection between mind and body (see Embody, see p. 119).

Tips for a successful practice

- ✧ Give yourself space. Allow enough time to prepare and process alone. If you attend a sports game, group class or workshop, don't hang about chatting after. If the activity is in the evening, give yourself enough time to rest before and reflect afterwards before going to bed. If you are sharing an activity with a friend, remember this day is about you finding your flow, not helping your companion(s) find theirs.

- ✧ Look after yourself. Move steadily, challenge yourself just enough and rest when you need. Bring energising snacks and lots of water with you, whatever you do. If your retreat involves going out, keep your phone with you for safety if you need to but keep it switched off. This retreat day is about losing your sense of time and self-consciousness in order to get your creative flow going again, not making a visual record to show your friends afterwards, or allowing yourself to be distracted.

- ✧ Let go of perfection. Once you're in your flow state, your skill will naturally improve. Perhaps put on music you love to help you flow during appropriate activities. Know that not everyone will experience flow in the same way. Don't beat yourself up if you don't feel yourself access yours – you will probably have a better idea, after today, of what might help you access it next time.

- ✧ Go back to being a child. If you're stuck as to what activity to choose, think back to what you loved doing when you were around nine or ten, just before you reached puberty. Childhood play often involves spontaneous flow, and reconnecting with those activities can help us access our flow state again as an adult. What were your main interests and passions? What did you love doing most in your free time? How might you adapt these things to your life today? If you can't remember what you loved – and a shocking number of us can't – ask your parent(s) or someone who knew you well what it was.

Reflect on your practice

After your retreat day, allow yourself time to rest and recover. If time and budget allow, maybe have a massage to reward yourself for your efforts and ease any tired muscles. Write in your journal how you felt, and which activity you might do again, or would do differently next time. What did you find most challenging, and why do you think that is? Which activity resonated with you the most? Do you have more or less energy, or creativity, to tackle something with which you were struggling yesterday?

Continue your practice

Once you find an activity you love that truly absorbs you, it won't feel like an effort to keep doing it. It will become a healthy fixation, one that you want to return to again and again because it gives you joy and truly relaxes you. Keep challenging yourself and you will build up your strength, stamina and resilience over time, and be more able to access your creative self on a regular basis.

Retreats to help you find your flow

Hosted retreats are ideal ways to push your boundaries in a safe environment. Go to be alongside like-minded others who also love your chosen activity, or to try something new to see if it helps you find your flow – whether you're throwing a pot in a studio, horse-riding across a beach, reading on a retreat in the countryside or singing in a group on a Mediterranean isle. Yoga holidays that mix activities such as stand-up paddleboarding, skiing, climbing or wild swimming can be a particularly fun way to access your flow state while also looking after yourself.

RETREAT FOR LONGER
BE AN ARTIST

Have you ever seen yourself as an artist? An artist can be anyone who creates art as a profession or hobby, from sculptor to musician, or who is accomplished at a task – you might be a landscape artist, but you might also be an artist in the kitchen. Artists pay attention, follow sparks and shape something that didn't exist before. They see the world, feel something about it and respond by creating. Skill can be taught and honed, but feeling and curiosity lead the way.

Neuroscientist Dr Kelly Lambert focuses on the 'effort-driven rewards' that come from engaging in such meaningful, hands-on creative activities in her book *Lifting Depression*. Doing things that produce 'a result you can see, feel, and touch – such as knitting a sweater or tending a garden', she says, enhances our mental wellbeing and boosts our confidence and resilience. It really doesn't matter if you're an expert or not.

Do you already have a way of being an artist in your life, or are you yearning to start something? Making something, and experiencing the results, floods our bodies with feel-good hormones and gives us a renewed thirst to keep being creative.

Take time out to create something

I suggest taking three days for this retreat, but feel free to make it longer if you choose, taking more time for each process. Gather what you need at least a week before you start. Day one is a warm up, where you go out and find visual beauty on your own terms, then return to create something in response to it – see below for ideas on how to find beauty. Day two is time to try something creative that's new to you – see below for ideas of projects to pick. Day three is to finish up, relax and process what you have experienced.

How to find beauty

Start by asking yourself – what does beauty mean to you, and what is beautiful to you? What you find visually beautiful will be highly personal to you. Let your inner artist relax and be free in your search for it. Allow yourself to stare and be amazed. Looking out at something inspirational can be just as powerful as looking inwards when we are on retreat.

Your version of visual beauty, for example, could be the colour or pattern in a painting, or an objet d'art or a sculpture in a local art gallery, museum or historic building. An item from nature from somewhere local that has personal significance to you, such as a favourite beach, view point, riverbank or tree. The way light-infused water flows over the pebbles in a local stream, say, or the shell-pink petals and emerald-green stem of a peony.

Look up, especially if you are somewhere urban. You may be surprised at what you find. A piece of hard-hitting, vibrant graffiti on a wall; a hidden loft window graced by faded coloured shutters; an enclosed wrought-iron balcony blooming with a cascade of bougainvillea. Your beauty could be anywhere – in a baker's shop window, the way someone's coat or shawl moves as they walk down the street, the feel of a book cover or glass object in your hand. You choose.

Ideas for projects to pick

Writerly pursuits: On paper, sketch out the scenes for a film, or plan the plot of a non-fiction book, novella or novel. Start a TV or play script. Write something short, such as a story or a haiku (see A Pause For Haiku, p. 113). Prepare a personalised set of affirmation cards. Write letters to loved ones, or a speech for an upcoming family or friendship event. Plan an elaborate celebration.

Arty pursuits: Make collages from images you love, design personalised gift wraps, knit or crochet something colourful, sketch spontaneous ideas, or paint a lively scene. Try embroidery or felting, experiment with linocuts, create a mosaic, start a quilt, throw a pot, or fold origami.

Making pursuits: Make your own bath salts, scrubs or candles, or prepare your own set of tisanes or herb-infused oils, salts or vinegars. Brew your own kombucha, start your own kefir or sourdough, bake and decorate a splendidly ambitious cake, make a cotton or leather pouch, or piece of jewellery. Create your own herb garden or vegetable bed (see Garden, p. 74).

Make yourself the canvas: Book a session with a colour therapist to understand what colours truly suit your complexion, then sketch or plan an outfit for yourself afterwards. Dye your hair, paint your nails, design your own tattoo for a later date.

Decorate your home: Style a gallery of your favourite people on one of your walls. Create your own wallpaper. Paint a mural. Experiment with shifting objects and pictures around. Newly frame photos, or make or paint a box to put treasures in.

Nature pursuits: Take yourself outside to engage in nature-focused writing, photography, sketchbooking or crafting (see Garden, p. 74). Bring the outside in, from exquisite shells to smooth pebbles.

Musical pursuits: Compose your own piece of music, write the lyrics to a song, create a playlist to share with someone you love, or experiment with recording and mixing sounds.

Suggested schedule

Day one: Find and respond to beauty

On waking: Ask yourself, what is your personal definition of beauty? Write it down in your journal or on some loose paper, if you choose.

Morning: Go out somewhere you love, or you haven't explored before, to find your definition of 'beauty' in it. Take your time. No rush. Once you have identified something you find compelling, take pictures, sketch or doodle, record a voice note, take notes about it, or collect little things to take home.

Afternoon: On your return to your retreat space, create something small in response to the visual beauty you have found. You could write about it in a short piece of prose, dialogue or poem such as a haiku (see A Pause For Haiku, p. 113). Or you could create a piece of art with materials of your choice – a mini collage of photos or scrapbook of doodles, a pencil line drawing or a picture using traditional paints, or a plan for an area of your garden inspired by something you have seen. Whatever you find both achievable and inspirational.

Evening: Enjoy your evening meal, then relax in any way you choose. You could carry on with your afternoon activity, if you've found it restful. After, go for a short walk in the fresh evening air to separate yourself from your task and relax for the night ahead of you. Before sleep, picture the most beautiful thing you saw, wrote or made today in your mind's eye. Ask yourself, how does it make you feel?

Day two: Pursue a creative project

On waking: Try sketching from scratch, a fun exercise to begin a creative process that I learned from textile artist Erin Dale, on The Nest retreat in Cornwall, England.

Fetch a large piece of plain paper and a pencil, and sit by an open window. Look out at something that catches your eye. It could be a plant, a tree branch, a pot, light on a wall, the shape of a cloud in the sky, a bike wheel, a wheelie bin, anything goes. Place your pencil in a space on the blank page, then take a few minutes or more to sketch it, *without looking down at the page again.*

It doesn't matter what is happening on the page. What matters is that you are engaging with what you are looking at. When you feel you have 'finished', the results may make you chuckle, but that's beside the point. This is a great way to pay attention and to relax about how you feel 'doing art'.

Daytime: After breakfast, take the day to create something you have never made before. Aim to produce a result you can see, feel, touch or experience (see ideas for projects to pick, p. 109).

You could carry on with and embellish the project you began yesterday if it feels 'new' and absorbing enough. Or you could learn something new, as a beginner – by following an online tutorial or an artist's how-to book, or pre-booking a local class.

You could also pursue an existing creative hobby. Try something related to it you haven't done before – prepare a batch of healthy smoothies if you mainly bake, for example, or create handmade greeting cards if you usually draw portraits.

Whatever you choose, leave time and space in your schedule to prepare beforehand, rest in the middle, and reflect afterwards.

Evening: Before or after your meal, tidy your space so you have a feeling of completion. Take a walk in the fresh air or have a long soak in a bath to mark the day's end.

Day three: Complete and process

Keep your schedule free, so you can do today what you feel like doing to complete your retreat. Finish a project from day one or day two. Take time to process how you feel, and which things you might take forwards in your life. Look at what you have produced – feel it, and touch it. Rest, move, bathe and dream in between.

A PAUSE FOR HAIKU

Haikus can be a simple and satisfying way into writing a poem when you are on a retreat, and to connect with yourself and the world around you. A Japanese art form that has been evolving since the 1600s, these charming small poems are like word paintings, capturing a moment or experience in time, and many people, from children to grandparents, enjoy writing them.

Traditionally they follow a three-line structure, with a syllable pattern of 5-7-5, and draw on nature for inspiration. Contemporary haiku sometimes plays with the syllable pattern, and is written about anything at all, most especially the nuances of daily life.

Here's an untitled haiku by poet Amy Lowell:

Watching the iris,
the faint and fragile petals—
how am I worthy?

And here's a haiku I wrote about a train journey in Vietnam:

Hard Sleeper From Lào Cai

We sip Glenfiddich,
play cards barefoot on bamboo—
rain taps a tattoo.

You can see that anything goes. Begin by observing something that stirs you in your daily life. Write three lines that relate to that thing. Aim for simplicity and a contrast between two ideas or images. Play about until the first line has five syllables, the second seven, and the third five again. That's it!

Tips for a successful practice

- ✧ Personalise your projects to help motivate yourself. You could start a quilt in honour of someone you have lost if you like to sew, for example, or write a song or poem for someone precious to you in your life right now.

- ✧ Feel free to invite a trusted friend or family member to join you in your chosen pursuit on day two if you want to, but keep time to yourself for day one.

- ✧ Resist judging yourself, both while you are making your creations and when you take a look at the end result. The practice is the journey – something you create might 'not work', and you may end up throwing it away. That's okay. Remember, being creative is an act of bravery (for more on this, see Resources, p. 261).

Reflect on your practice

Soon after your retreat, take a look at your creations and check in with yourself. How do you feel when you see, touch, read or experience them? Is there anything you'd do differently next time, or perhaps be less perfectionistic about? Is there anything you'd like to carry on in a class, workshop or retreat? Is there anything else you'd like to try that you have not tried so far?

Continue your practice

Take yourself out regularly to find beauty: If you enjoyed going out and finding beauty on your own terms on day one, carry on with this and do other things like it on a regular basis, blocking out time in your calendar to do so, and keeping that time all to yourself.

Make your own art cupboard: If you take a fancy to artistic creation, one of the most compelling ways to enable yourself to create on a regular basis is to make your own art cupboard with things that inspire you. Your interpretation of 'cupboard' can be loose, however. It can be as simple as a case with coloured pencils in it, or you could devote a drawer or dresser to art and add to it paints of all kinds, a mixing palette, charcoals, ribbons, origami paper, pads of paper and so on.

Join a class: Pick your project and book yourself into a weekly in-person local class to help you hone your craft, then consider finding people you respect and trust with whom you can form a regular club. You could also try an online class or workshop, so you can enjoy it in the peace and quiet of your chosen retreat space (see Resources, p. 261).

Involve your family: Sometimes, as a family, we have Sunday art sessions after breakfast – you can do this at home at low or no cost. My daughter picks a theme and our chosen materials, and we sit around our kitchen table and each create a different response to the theme. Then, just for fun, we comment on them and mark them out of ten. Sometimes we keep what we've created, sometimes it goes in the bin. What matters is that we've had a laugh, and feel relaxed and connected. My brother Chris and his family once took the month of January to each write and share a daily haiku for each other (see A Pause For Haiku, p. 113). This is an especially good way to stay connected if you have children who are now young adults and no longer live with you.

Hosted creative retreats

There are lots of hosted retreats available for the creatively curious that pivot around different themes, from painting, bookbinding, furniture making and crafting to photography, pottery and writing of all kinds. Go on these to improve your skills in something you love, or learn something new from scratch in a nurturing space with like-minded others. You'll be free of domestic tasks, with an expert on tap to help you hone your craft, and you'll more often than not have a lot of lovely fun. Check ahead that the skill level and theme suit your needs. A 'writing retreat' where most guests are working on a memoir while you want to workshop a novel, for example, will not serve you well. Some special retreats also offer quiet, serviced spaces where you can complete a creative work in progress.

NURTURE

On Days When
you feel like a wilting garden,
gather yourself, roll up your lawn,
bouquet your flowers,
embrace your weeds

Dean Atta

How do you nurture yourself? When we care for ourselves as well as others, we feel more balanced, confident, and better able to handle daily stress. Nurturing doesn't have to be dramatic; it can happen quietly, in small steps. A self-devised retreat is a perfect space in which to practise.

Nurturing involves tuning in to what we need, and responding with small, consistent gestures. It's not always easy, as we're often taught from a young age to cope – or pretend to – and keep going. But when we climb into a nest we've made and gift ourselves care, magical things can happen.

Creating a regular movement practice, having a 'treat' day, or resting deeply all help us emerge recharged, ready to meet life with fresh energy.

How much time do you have to retreat?

- ✧ An hour – Embody (p. 119)
- ✧ A day – Treat yourself (p. 126)
- ✧ Longer – Stay put (p. 134)

Whatever you choose, refer to the Retreat Toolkit (p. 15) to help you prepare for each retreat.

Start with a check-in

Write in your journal or think to yourself:

- ✧ *When I'm feeling jaded, at my desk or during chores, I usually . . .*
- ✧ *The idea of pampering myself makes me feel . . .*
- ✧ *When I feel exhausted in my everyday life, I tend to . . .*

RETREAT FOR AN HOUR
EMBODY

The word 'embody' comes from the Latin *in corpus* – literally, 'in body' – and it means to give a tangible form to an idea, quality or feeling. In the context of holistic exercise, it involves fully inhabiting your body and mind while you move, bringing your whole self into a practice.

When was the last time you moved consciously, with your mind alert to what you were physically doing? When we practise embodied movement, we are not just 'going through the motions', with music blaring and our mind on other things. Connected to our breath, and moving our body with intention, we are fully present and focused. As my Iyengar Yoga teacher in Australia, Glenn Ceresoli, says: 'Unless we focus on our breath during our practice, and being in the moment, we are just stretching.'

Moving in this way leaves us relaxed as well as alert, because it activates the parasympathetic nervous system, the part of us that's responsible for rest, digestion and recovery. It does the opposite to the sympathetic nervous system, which prepares us for action or danger – the so-called 'fight or flight' response.

There are many holistic practices to choose from. The key thing is to bring both your mind and body into your choice. When we do, it's difficult to be anywhere else other than in the moment.

Embodied movement:

- Activates the body's relaxation response.
- Energises the body and boosts circulation.
- Acts as a form of Meditation in motion.
- Provides an uplifting start or break to the day.

- Helps shift energy when we're feeling tired or sluggish.
- Helps release blocked emotions.

Take an hour to move holistically

Choose a way to move for your retreat hour that brings together movement, breath and focused awareness to nourish your body and mind. Start with something you can do easily in your own space, without any props or guidance, or look for a local class to attend or an online session to follow.

If you are new to a practice, it's best to learn in person. If you already have a regular practice, why not shake things up and try something else for your retreat hour? Whatever you choose, wear appropriate clothing, hydrate before you start and give yourself time to rest for a few moments after. Then head into the rest of your day more energised, relaxed and focused.

Ideas for ways to move holistically

Without guidance

- **Mindful, steady walking:** Best done outdoors, ideally in nature, but your local streets or a nearby park work too. Early morning is a particularly gorgeous time to see your area in a different light. Walk at a steady pace of your choice, matching your breath to your strides, noticing the sensations in your body and the rhythm of your steps (see A Pause For Walking, p. 30).

- **Mindful, steady swimming:** Find a quiet pool where you can swim uninterrupted laps, or choose a stretch of safe, wild water. Swim using your favourite stroke at a relaxed pace of your choice, focusing on your breath and the feeling of the water on your skin. This is a full-body workout that clears the mind through steady repetition and builds physical endurance.

- **Intuitive stretching:** Do anywhere you have space to move freely. Start slowly, breathing as you move, stretching out whatever part of you feels stiff in that moment. This is a gentle way to release stiffness, improve flexibility and connect with your body's needs.

- **Freeform dance:** Find a private space where you can move freely. Play music you love to keep you in the zone. Let your breath and body guide your pace, and move in whatever way feels right in the moment, with no rules. This is a full-body release that lifts your mood, raises your heart rate and helps you feel fully alive. As Gerald the Giraffe says in one of my favourite children's books, *Giraffes Can't Dance* by Giles Andreae: 'We all can dance . . . when we find music that we love.'

With guidance

If you're a beginner and don't want to leave your chosen retreat space for this hour, Qigong is the easiest practice to try by following an online session. For the other practices below, it's best to seek out an in-person class unless you are familiar with them (see Resources, p. 261).

Qigong: The Chinese medicinal practice of Qigong (pronounced chee-gong) uses breath and mindful movement to help you cultivate a strong, balanced Qi, otherwise known as your life force or vital energy. This is the easiest of the guidance practices to try if you want to stay in your chosen retreat space for your retreat hour, because it's gentle on most bodies, simple to learn, and can be practised in short, standalone exercises as well as a continuous sequence of movements.

Tai Chi: Qigong's close sibling features sequences of meditative, flowing movements that you practise slowly and mindfully, to develop balance, coordination and internal awareness. Originally developed as a martial art, it includes self-defence techniques.

Somatic movement: Body-based awareness practices of various kinds that encourage conscious focus on internal sensations during movement – on how the body feels, rather than how it looks or performs.

Pilates: Created by Joseph Pilates to help rehabilitate sick and wounded soldiers during the First World War, this practice became popular with dancers to prevent injury before it entered the mainstream. Its core exercises link movement, breath and body awareness to rebuild, align, strengthen and tone. Stay totally in your body and with your breath to lift your movement out of 'exercise' and into embodiment.

Ecstatic dance: A free-form, unchoreographed group dance practice usually experienced in a supportive group setting, led by a teacher or a DJ. Once you get over any initial inhibitions, it can leave you feeling joyful, free and deeply connected to yourself and others.

A PAUSE FOR YOGA

Yoga is a classic and extremely popular embodied movement practice that enables you to reclaim mind, body and soul on a regular basis. It builds strength, balance and flexibility through *asanas* (physical postures), while *pranayama* (yogic breathwork) helps to settle the nervous system and integrate the mind and body (see Breathe, p. 191).

It's important, if you are a beginner, that you learn Yoga in person, with a fully trained and trusted teacher, rather than in an online class. This is because your teacher can provide immediate feedback, ensure safety by preventing injury, and offer personalised guidance tailored to your needs. This strong foundation sets you up for confident, successful progress as you continue learning the practice (see Resources, p. 261).

Be prepared to experiment with different teachers and classes before you find 'your thing'. Styles range from gentle alignment-focused types, like Hatha and Iyengar, to slow, deep-stretch practices like Yin, dynamic flows such as Vinyasa and Ashtanga, and spiritually-oriented forms like Kundalini and Jivamukti, which combine vigorous movement with a focus on spiritual philosophy.

After a course of lessons, you could start your own Yoga practice at home. Ask a teacher you trust to jot down a short routine on paper for you to start with. Over time, you can adapt and expand your practice as you learn and your body changes. My daily Yoga practice looks very different now to when I first learned Yoga in my twenties.

Bear in mind that physical postures are only a part of Yoga, which comes from the Veda – the ancient body of knowledge that is also the source of Vedic Meditation (see De-excite, p. 163) and Ayurveda (see Refresh yourself, p. 51). The word *Yoga* means 'to join', and its ultimate purpose is to help us realise the unity between our small self and a greater consciousness which yogis believe connects us all. Traditionally, *asanas* were a way to prepare the body to sit for Vedic Meditation and access this blissful union. Something to build up to?

Tips for a successful practice

- ✧ Whatever you choose, move naturally and within your comfort zone, keeping your breathing relaxed.
- ✧ Adjust the movements to suit your body. You might use controlled movements to protect your joints, while hypermobile bodies can activate the core to prevent overextension. If you're stiff, start with smaller movements and gradually increase their range.
- ✧ Afterwards, take proper time to hydrate and rest.

Reflect on your practice

Notice the quality of presence you have cultivated, and how your body feels during the rest of the day. Then, during the rest of your week, if you find some time, do your chosen practice again or try a different one, and check in to see how you feel after. Is this something you might want to make part of your regular routine?

Continue your practice

Embodied movement is a perfect way to start your morning, or it can be used to pep yourself up whenever you need it during your day. If you'd like a practice to take with you into the rest of your life, experiment until you find the one that suits you best, trying out different classes and workshops.

To get into the discipline of a regular practice, commit to doing a few key movements, then slowly build up to more. Invest in a mat if you don't have one. To make it easier to get into a habit, you could lay your mat out the night before and go straight to it in the morning.

You don't have to take a full hour – even 15 mins of embodied movement each day will make a difference. Note that listening to, and making, sound can also be forms of embodiment (See A Pause For Sound, p. 104).

Hosted embodied movement retreats

There are oodles of lovely hosted retreats that feature Qigong, Tai Chi, Pilates, Yoga, Somatic movement, dance and other embodied movement practices to help you relax, rebalance and get fitter. The best are held in gorgeous natural locations and include healthy, nutritious meals and downtime. Take time to research the teacher, who will be key to a successful retreat. The most effective teachers will draw on the depth of their own practice and life experience, in addition to having a sound knowledge of anatomy, to help you move in the right way for your body.

RETREAT FOR A DAY
TREAT YOURSELF

What feels like a 'treat' to you? It could be smelling fragrant roses, basking in a sauna or sipping a flute of champagne. But it could also be a reassuring reminder to yourself, such as saying 'this too will pass' as you head into a meeting you don't want to attend. In our society, the idea of 'treating yourself' is seen by some as unnecessary and indulgent, but while life can be testing and chaotic, how you treat yourself during it matters.

The word treat and retreat come from the same Latin root, *trahere*, meaning 'to pull'. While 'retreat' means to pull back or withdraw, 'treat' can mean to pull something towards you by attending to it. To treat yourself is an act of care and self-respect, and it can mean many things in the context of retreating: allowing yourself to indulge in pleasure and delight; how you think about and behave towards yourself; and the steps you take to deal with an injury, condition or illness you might have.

A retreat is a form of treat. It's something restorative and nurturing you can offer yourself by withdrawing from routine or stress, which makes it a fitting time to indulge in small practices of self-care, so you can live your life with joy and strength. And why not? It's not as if we get out of life alive, as the saying goes. We may as well make the best of it.

Allow yourself a treat day

Decide how you are going to treat yourself during your day in advance, so you can be prepared. You might pick one thing for each part of your day, to do in the early morning, mid-morning, afternoon and evening (see suggestions below). Save a little, so as to gift yourself something luscious you wouldn't usually buy – even something as small as a food-related treat can lift you. If you'd like a treatment, take time to find and book someone local who could come to your home, or who practises in a restful environment. Grace your home beforehand with things that bring you joy, whether that's a vase of fresh flowers or a new book to flick through.

Suggestions for what to do on your treat day

Pamper yourself: Let's start with the fluffy and the frivolous. Surround yourself with things that soothe and delight. Drape yourself with soft things and waft about your home. Dim the lights. Add more pillows to your bed, and cushions to your sofa. Flick through a gorgeous picture book with no aim. Relish the warmth of a heated blanket, or a cashmere shawl. Spray your face with a facial mist. Use the 'good' skincare products you've been saving.

Choose maximalism: Retreating doesn't have to feel puritanical. Bring back the hedonistic side of life, and lean into pleasure and playful excess. What might that look like for you? You could dress yourself in bold colours and rich textures. Choose the loveliest jumper, one you've been saving perhaps, over the one you always wear. Novels over newsletters. Piano or reggae over muzak. The embossed notebook still in its box over the reporter's one made of card. Or vice versa, because to treat yourself is to give yourself permission to find pleasure on your own terms.

Feast and sip: Follow the 80/20 rule – mostly nourishing foods, with space for treats you love. Relish the artisan chocolate, coffee, wine or homemade cake. Help yourself to seconds. Add a touch of celebration with a mock- or cocktail of your choice. Savour your favourites mindfully.

Pick out a present: Enjoy a mooch around the shops today and buy yourself a small present of something you've longed for to look at, adorn yourself with, wear or eat. It's not called retail 'therapy' for nothing. Or take yourself outside to pick a gift from nature – the smoothest pebble, the palest petals to press, a pretty shell that fits in your palm. Or plant something bright you can watch bursting into life next season – a vibrant red poppy in an empty bed, or an array of yellow irises in a pot (see Garden, p. 74).

Bathe: One of the loveliest ways to retreat quickly into your own world, bathing has been an act of solace for centuries. It calms the nervous system, relieves aches and pains, boosts circulation, aids sleep, lowers blood pressure, clears out blocked sinuses and much more. Run a deep bath and add generous amounts of relaxing essential oils, herbs or salts. Allow yourself an unhurried, soothing soak while you read a paperback, listen to an audio book, treat your skin to a face mask, breathe deeply, enjoy a cup of tea, or just close your eyes and dream. One of my favourite moments is after the bath, when I'm unfurled and cooling down – the Japanese call this *yuagari*. Keep a notebook nearby – as creators from Archimedes to Virginia Woolf have known, many great ideas have surfaced in the bath. For more on getting the most out of your bath, see Resources, p. 261.

Relish aroma: Smell is our most immediate sense to indulge. As gardener Beverley Nichols wrote, 'to be overcome by the fragrance of flowers is a delectable form of defeat'. Enjoy aromatic flowers, oils, candles and teas today. Use lavender to soothe, lemon balm to lift, bergamot and rose to ease tension, frankincense to ground you, and jasmine for its heady, optimistic perfume.

Savour touch: Touch is the first sense we develop in the womb, and it's an easy way to regulate our nervous system. Comforting touch, like hand-holding, lowers stress hormones and releases oxytocin, promoting a sense of safety and calm. Gift it to yourself today through hugging, hand-holding, sexual connection, or even dancing barefoot with someone you love. Share a simple massage with a friend or family member, or ease the tension in your own shoulders, calves and feet with a natural oil like almond or coconut.

Embrace treatments: Having a treatment with an excellent therapist is a retreat in itself, and a 'treat' day is a fitting time to indulge in one. Full body massages, soothing facials, body scrubs and wraps can be wonderfully rejuvenating in the right hands. Or book rebalancing bodywork or another holistic therapy to steady the nervous system, reduce stress and support your body's natural repair processes. My favourites are reflexology, shiatsu and sound healing (see A Pause For Sound, p. 104). My regular go-to is acupuncture, which always brings release and renews my feelings of hope, which is why it inspired my poem 'Acupuncture' (see p. 273).

Tend to what hurts: To treat also means to heal, so if you have a physical or emotional issue that's been niggling you, take today to start to do something about it. Where do you feel tension, discomfort or depletion? Let that be your guide. If your feet are worse for wear, see a chiropodist rather than relying on a pedicure. Don't ignore the knee pain stopping you jogging – seek out a physio. If sadness, grief or anxiety are lingering, take time to research a therapist who can help. For guidance in finding the right person, see Resources, p. 261.

Talk to yourself kindly: How we speak to ourselves matters. The words we use can expand or limit our sense of self, shaping our thoughts and how we live. Today, notice your inner voice – is it judging, nagging or criticising you? Turn that around, and speak to yourself with love and patience. As we learn how to be kind to ourselves, we model it for our children too.

Many of us have learned to think about ourselves from a place of fear or self-protection, but we can choose otherwise. Loneliness can signal the need to reach out – to others or to ourselves (see A Pause For Befriending, p. 90). Try creating a praise album, filled with confidence boosts others have sent to you over time, or make these part of your own field guide to life (see Practise self-reliance, p. 152). Add yourself to a gratitude list (see Choose gratitude, p. 146), create some positive affirmations for yourself (see Affirm, p. 143), or try simply shrugging, smiling and letting things go more often (see A Pause For Letting Go, below).

Suggested schedule

Morning: Light a candle, mist your face and wrap yourself in something soft before doing any regular practice you might have – or not. Make a gratitude list, using the luxurious notebook you've been saving if you have one. Include things about yourself and your life you genuinely love. Wallow beautifully for the rest of the morning, pausing for treats.

Afternoon: Prepare a satisfying lunch and enjoy it slowly, or eat out somewhere you adore. Go shopping or for a walk in nature to pick out a gift for yourself. Have a long, indulgent or healing treatment. Take a bath and sip champagne, a cup of tea or an infusion of fresh lemon balm or mint. Settle into bed with yourself or your companion.

Evening: Enjoy a comforting meal alone or with a loved one. Lay the table with care – a fresh cloth, a vase of flowers. Have an evening treatment by candlelight. Dance under the moon with a friend. Bolster your bed with extra cushions, mist your sheets with fragrance, read a witty novel and follow your breath into rest.

A PAUSE FOR LETTING GO

Ask most people what they'd like from life and their reply is likely to involve the word 'happiness', but this isn't a permanent state of being. It's our natural state to have changing emotions, and allowing ourselves to feel the full force of them is what makes us human. Anxiety, guilt, nervousness, anger, disappointment, even a general feeling of boredom, are all legitimate reactions to the situations life throws at us. We can learn how to alleviate and work through them, but we won't ever be able to banish them from our roster of feelings.

A better response might be to let things go: an art linked to the Buddhist concept of non-attachment. Rather than clinging to thoughts, feelings, possessions, people and all the 'shoulds' we carry around in life, the idea is to practise letting them go and accepting things, and ourselves, as they are. When we stop clinging to who we think we should be, and instead meet ourselves with compassion and humour, loneliness and sorrow no longer feel like threats.

Why not let go of excessive worry, social pressures, self-improvement, connections that don't serve you, reaching for distraction, situations over which we have no control, and the endless loop of overthinking? A modern, cheeky twist to the Buddhist theory of non-attachment is to just say 'fuck it'. Popularised as a retreat practice by founders of the irreverent 'Fuck It Life' movement, John C. Parkin and Gaia Pollini, the phrase helps us quickly drop what doesn't matter and focus on what does. It often works for me.

Tips for a successful practice

- ✦ This is a treat day – anything goes. Don't put any pressure on yourself, or try to make it perfect. The point is to feel good, not to try to 'grow'.
- ✦ Allow your mood to lead the way, and if your plans shift, let them. Comfort, pleasure and kindness are the only measures of success today.

Reflect on your practice

The morning after your treat day, ask yourself what you loved, and what you wish you'd done that you didn't. Take something forwards – a scent, a snack, a slower pace, a kind word for yourself – and make space for another treat in the following days or weeks.

Continue your practice

Let your treat day be a beginning, not a one-off. Keep treating yourself regularly, and treating yourself well. Things you start today can evolve – speak to yourself with more kindness, extend your gratitude list, grow your praise album, let go of things you are holding onto, book that next massage, or a course of them.

Weave small, joyful rituals into each day. Treating yourself doesn't have to take hours. Channel your inner Emily from Frances Hodgson Burnett's novel *The Making of a Marchioness*: 'Can you give me five minutes to lie down quite flat and dab my forehead with eau de Cologne?'

Step up for yourself if something deeper is troubling you. For support with long-standing emotional issues, such as anxiety, grief or depression, research counsellors who can help you work things through and start to make lasting changes.

Hosted retreats for treats and treatment

There are many reliable health retreats in beautiful locations around the globe that are devoted to your care, comfort and recovery. Whether you are looking for indulgence or intervention, the best are in rejuvenating settings away from the world, and run by a team of experts. Try a private or family counselling retreat for therapy, a medical health retreat for help with an injury or to recover after an illness, or go to places that have access to natural hot springs of mineral-rich waters, so you can experience a proper 'spa' retreat. The word 'spa' stands for the Latin *sanus per aquam*, which means 'health through water', and you can find thermal spa retreats across Europe, especially in Italy, Switzerland and Iceland, or by staying at a *ryokan* near one of the fabulous *onsens* in Japan. For help with letting go, try a Buddhist retreat (see p. 216) or a Fuck It retreat (thefuckitlife.com).

RETREAT FOR LONGER
STAY PUT

Do you, like me, find holiday planning a little stressful? Sometimes staying home feels much easier. We often pin big hopes on summer and winter breaks, yet the effort of researching, booking, packing and travelling can outweigh the reward. Why not turn staying put into a retreat instead? A chance to nurture yourself – and your family – away from the hustle and bustle.

We're quite used to the idea of hibernation in winter, when animals such as bats, hedgehogs and brown bears enjoy a deliciously long nap out of the cold. We often mimic them by staying in more ourselves. Other animals, particularly in hot, dusty countries, enter a similar state in the summer instead, to avoid extreme heat and drought, a process scientists call 'aestivation'.

We go on holiday to escape the familiar – but we can turn that familiar into something that serves us, by choosing to stay home to rest and regroup, and make like the animals do. Many of us are so exhausted, yet the pressure to work, achieve and keep going never stops. Is it time to step off the carousel and sink into rest? Whether that means embracing winter's darkness and quiet, or relishing the expansive heat and light of summer.

Take time out to aestivate or hibernate

If you're in summer, aestivate. If you're nearing winter, hibernate. A weekend is a good start, but ideally take a week, ten days, a fortnight or even a whole delicious month. Pledge to be idle as often as possible. Encourage your family to join you, turning your hibernation or aestivation into a mix of restful time alone and together.

Lean into the idea of *being*, and take away as much of the *doing* as you can. Just like the bear or the crocodile, you are slowing down and resting, not trying to grow or change. Instead, question how you can rest deeply, to replenish mind and body, within your house and local area.

Suggestions for what to do when you stay put

Add a daily dose of joy: Do things regularly that boost your mood and absorb you in a comfortable way. Put your feet up and listen to music you love or an interesting podcast, or indulge in reading (see A Pause For Reading, p. 29). Give yourself or a family member a mini facial or foot massage, book a treatment (see Treat yourself, p. 126), reconnect with your dreams by journalling (see Journal, p. 69), or get creative (see Be an artist, p. 108).

Rest: During the day, mimic the deep-rest environment of the cave and the womb by lying down, ideally in the dark, and covering yourself with a warm blanket or shawl. Rest on your bed, or a mat, with cushions under your head and knees to support your spine, and cover your eyes with an eye mask or light scarf. Or simply sit, cover your eyes and let your body settle, inviting tension to release and rest to begin (see De-excite, p. 163).

Sleep: Do as the dormouse and desert tortoise do and gift yourself the chance of decent sleep throughout your hibernation or aestivation. At first, ignore all the rules and allow yourself to catch up on sleep, indulging in lie-ins, siestas and going to bed super early if you feel like it. But then start to get your sleep into a better schedule (See A Pause For Sleep, p. 137).

Befriend your body clock: Once you've caught up on sleep, use this time to tune into natural circadian rhythms and gently reset your body clock if you feel out of sync. Guided by light, this 24-hour system regulates sleep, energy, mood, hormones and temperature – so aligning with it restores balance. Ideally, wake with the sun, sleep when it sets and eat your main meal at midday. If that feels out of reach, simply shift bedtimes, waking times and meals a little earlier each day of your retreat, to ease into a healthier rhythm for everyday life.

Potter: There's a wonderful art to pottering, and this is the perfect time to indulge it. Fiddle and fold, move things about, tidy a little. Drift from bed to tea, to putting on a wash, to gazing out a window, to stepping into your garden to notice what's growing. Make the most of being at home – perhaps in fresh pyjamas or barefoot, enjoying the feel of floors or grass. Pottering is tending gently – watering a plant, sorting fresh laundry, washing fruit with care. Such quiet, slow rituals become meditative and honour your home (see Be mindful, p. 199).

Bask: Bask in warmth, water or the wild – at home or nearby, depending on the season. In summer, sunbathe safely, walk or cycle in nature, forest bathe (see Be mindful p. 199), or swim in the sea, river, lake or a pool (see Refresh yourself, p. 51). Then end the day watching the light fade, or moving gently in a space you love (see Embody, p. 119). In winter, book a sauna or steam, enjoy home comforts, or take a long bath (see Treat yourself, p. 126). Cocooned in blankets, relish firelight or starlight.

Suggested schedule

One day on your own stay-put retreat might look like this:

Morning: Sleep in as long as you need – no alarm. Tune into your body (see De-excite, p. 163) or meditate, then make a hot drink. Journal to check in with yourself or write free-flow to offload (see Clear your mind, p. 47). Shower and enjoy a late breakfast, alone or with your family. Then move – perhaps a long walk in nature, some gardening, or gentle freeform movement indoors.

Afternoon: Make lunch your main meal, cooking it slowly, maybe with family if they'd like to join. Afterwards, rest –

meditate, have a siesta, or lie down in the dark. Read, draw, paint, or simply dream on a hammock in the garden. Potter gently, tending to small tasks like watering your plants or folding clothes.

Evening: Have an early, simple meal. Then choose how to close the day – a walk, reading, sketching, or a film. Light candles, cocoon in blankets, star gaze, sit around a fire with camomile tea or a glass of something stronger. Offer mini foot massages, and finish with deep, slow breathing before settling into bed.

A PAUSE FOR SLEEP

Good sleep is essential, because it boosts memory and focus, steadies your mood, strengthens your immune system and restores energy for overall health. But you may find that, like me, your sleep is the first thing to be disrupted if you're feeling off kilter. There are oodles of experts around the globe full of advice on how you can sleep better. Sleep tips that have worked for me consistently over the years, that I've discovered on various sleep-focused retreats, include:

- Go to bed and get up at the same time, even at weekends.

- If you can, make your bedroom a sleep sanctuary, and use it for very little else. Make sure it's dark, cool and quiet – I use blackout blinds.

- Have a wind-down routine each night, such as having a hot bath, reading something comforting, or light breathwork (see Breathe, p. 191).

- Switch off all screens and lower bright lights before bed. Some people say switch off for at least an hour before lights out, but I recommend you make it two or three.

- Follow a guided Yoga Nidra, a form of deep, conscious relaxation that readies you for sleep.

- Ask someone to read you a story, or listen to an audio book or pre-sleep podcast. Bedtime stories don't have to be just for children. Having someone read to you helps you relax, reduces mental effort, distracts from stress and creates a sleep-associated routine.

- Write a Worry List to offload any anxieties you may have before sleep, or in the night when you wake (see Clear your mind, p. 47).

- If you wake and can't get back to sleep, get up, wrap yourself up warm, make a camomile tea or similar, sip it while breathing in fresh air at an open door or window, then perhaps read something untaxing or add to your Worry List in low lighting, until you feel tired enough to go back to bed.

- Alternatively, dress warmly and try a few restorative Yoga poses to relax the body and calm the mind. Viparita Karani is a gentle inversion where you lie on your back and extend your legs vertically up against a wall, relaxing and breathing normally for a few minutes or more.

- If you are truly struggling, see your doctor or a sleep specialist. I also recommend learning Vedic Meditation as a daily practice, which has shifted my sleep routine entirely (see De-excite, p. 163).

Tips for a successful practice

- Be positive about staying put. As Austrian poet and novelist Rainer Maria Rilke says: 'It is very important to be idle with confidence, with devotion, possibly even with joy.'

- Schedule your day lightly, and allow yourself to go off piste. Rest doesn't mean total inactivity – if you were asked to lie down all day, you'd probably feel restless. You might prefer to go for a run or walk in nature first, and then lie down.

- Ideally, keep all your electronic devices off, especially if you are only 'staying put' for a weekend. Otherwise, manage your use of these devices, and your interaction with others, so you are not pulled off in lots of different directions (see Digital resistance, p. 37).

- If you want a massage or holistic therapy, perhaps start your retreat with one, then leave the rest of your time free so it can unfold with no commitments.

Reflect on your practice

A few days after your retreat, ask yourself, what one thing did I do during my hibernation or aestivation that truly worked for me? Practise it during the following week to help ease yourself back into life. It might be allowing yourself to potter in the evening, rather than saying yes to an invite out, or lying down in the dark as soon as you return from work each day.

Continue your practice

Are there easy, nurturing practices from this retreat that you can take forwards into each day, from taking time to potter and bask, to acts that gently prioritise sleep? Pick what has worked for you (and your family, if you have retreated with them), and set the intention to commit to them regularly. Being able to stay put and be still in daily life is an essential skill, as great thinkers have known for centuries.

Hosted retreats where you can stay put

If you find it difficult to stay in one place and truly rest in your own space, allow yourself a journey to a retreat. For deep rest, you might try a health retreat with a dedicated sleep programme to help you get to the bottom of issues such as insomnia, or a general wellness programme to gently rebalance your nervous system.

Long-stay retreats at health resorts around the world will help you truly indulge in your hibernation or aestivation in the care of others. A twenty-one-day Panchakarma programme at an Ayurveda retreat, for example, draws out all your tiredness so you cannot help but stop (see Refresh yourself, p. 51).

Staying put can also involve escaping traditional celebratory periods. While you might aestivate at home to avoid summer holiday crowds, you could consider going on a retreat to escape the winter festive period. Christmas and New Year retreats around the globe, for example, offer you peace, quiet and restorative practices if you want to avoid lots of socialising or overdoing food and drink.

TRUST

'we may safely trust a good deal more than we do'
Henry David Thoreau, Walden

Who and what do you trust in your life? Trust is essential to our wellbeing. The belief in the reliability, or truth, of someone or something, it lays the groundwork for healthy relationships, eases anxiety and loneliness, and fosters confidence and resilience.

For many of us, trusting doesn't come easily. Betrayal, mistreatment or low self-worth can make us doubt ourselves and others. Relentless negative news fuels fear and anxiety. Yet when we trust ourselves, the process of life, and other people, we often make better choices and move through change feeling safer and more connected.

Trusting can take work, but it need not be hard work. Simple retreat practices, done often, can help us sift through the noise and see what and who we can rely on. When we stay open, know our people and have confidence in ourselves, daily living gets easier.

How much time do you have to retreat?

- An hour – Affirm (p. 143)
- A day – Choose gratitude (p. 146)
- Longer – Practise self-reliance (p. 152)

Whatever you choose, refer to the Retreat Toolkit (p. 15) to help you prepare for each retreat.

Start with a check-in

Write in your journal or think to yourself:

- *I like to feel in control/go with the flow in life because . . .*
- *A person in the recent or distant past who supported me is . . .*
- *I find it challenging/easy to trust my own judgement because . . .*

RETREAT FOR AN HOUR

AFFIRM

Affirmations reframe unhelpful thoughts, feelings, attitudes or habits with intentions that foster trust – in ourselves, in others, in nature and in the unfolding process of life. From the Latin *affirmare*, meaning 'to make steady and strengthen', they are positive, suggestive phrases that help us let go of the need to control, and instead feel safe and confident about what lies ahead. They reshape our self-talk, rewiring the brain through repetition, to influence the way we think.

Used in spiritual and philosophical traditions for thousands of years, affirmations were popularised in the early twentieth century by French psychologist Émile Coué and his method of 'autosuggestion'. He created the affirmation 'Every day, in every way, I am getting better and better' for his patients, after observing that many improved more quickly when they expected to recover, encouraging them to trust in their own capacity for growth and healing.

Affirmations often start with 'I', then go on to state a desired outcome, such as 'I am a good friend', 'I am enough', or 'I choose to rest when I need to'. They're personal and yours to shape, repeat and refresh whenever you need. They help you move with, rather than against, the process of life.

Affirmations:

- Remind us what matters, especially when things feel fearful or stressful.
- Improve focus by keeping your mind on what you want to achieve.
- Boost self-confidence by easing our insecurities and fostering self-belief.

- Reduce anxiety by giving the mind something positive to think.

- Help motivate us to stick to our goals.

Take an hour to create an affirmation

Settle yourself somewhere comfortable, with your journal or loose paper. Ask yourself, what one thing do I need most in my daily life right now? Choose a phrase that resonates with this need, and write it down.

Close your eyes, take a breath and focus on your chosen phrase. Repeat it in your mind or aloud three times. Play with the wording until it feels right.

Decide how you will take this affirmation into your daily life. You could say it, write it, sing it, draw it, paint it, or read it from sticky notes around your retreat space. You could affirm with your eyes closed, whilst you look into your eyes in a mirror, or whilst you observe a favourite object or view.

When will you say it? It could be on waking, during a morning practice, at lunchtime, in an evening bath – once a day, three times a day, for a week or more. Choose what feels right at this time.

Then carry on with your day, with your affirmation ready to hand to help you when you need it.

Tips for a successful practice

- Your affirmation can be as specific or as broad, as long or as short, as you want, and it doesn't have to begin with 'I'. What matters is that the words feel grounding and true for you. 'I am strong enough to deal with my current family situation', or 'going to bed earlier is within reach'. Shorter affirmations can feel more powerful and easier to 'carry' with you.

- ✧ Make your affirmation feel attainable. If you're working through depression, 'I can feel moments of peace today' is going to be more realistic than 'I feel really happy'. Affirmations are not magic. If you say 'I am rich', it won't mean money is going to pour from your ceiling (a shame, I admit). But recast as 'I deserve abundance', it might just help you reframe your attitude to yourself and your work, and incrementally increase your earnings.

Reflect on your practice

Over the next few days, take a few moments to notice how your affirmation felt. Did the words bring comfort, energy or a sense of resistance? Over time, these small observations will help you refine affirmations that truly support and sustain you.

Continue your practice

Feel free to bring an affirmation practice into your daily life throughout your year, intermittently or regularly, as you need. Change your phrase to suit your current state and goals from week to week. Make phrases up to suit you in the moment, such as 'this too will pass' to help you get through something you don't want to do, or 'I can slow down' if you notice yourself rushing in traffic. Keep a few affirmations to return to when you need them. For example, 'I choose to respond with kindness, not react with anger' helps me with challenging work emails, while I use 'I am safe, all is well' to calm me when I'm feeling anxious. A few moments affirming a day, particularly during challenging periods or times of dramatic change, can have a powerful effect.

RETREAT FOR A DAY
CHOOSE GRATITUDE

Gratitude is the quality of being thankful. Woven into human life across traditions and cultures, it's a readiness to show appreciation for an experience, person or thing. Remembering who and what we are grateful for helps us build our trust in others and ourselves, and have faith in the flow of life. It can show us, especially when we feel disconnected, stressed or sad, that the universe has our back, that we can trust the natural world, and that other people, including strangers as well as friends, can often be there for us.

We can be grateful for anything – small or large, animal, vegetable or mineral, in our today or in our deep past. As natural as the heat of the sun, as small as a daisy growing out of a rock, as human as an unexpected hug from a child, as large as an astonishing giant sculpture in a public space, as comforting as the gift of a fireside on a stormy night.

When we're overwhelmed or feeling out of control, it's easy to shift into worry mode, focusing on what we lack or what's gone wrong, judging and criticising, creating mind clutter we can do without. By focusing on what we have and what's gone right, we step into a more manageable state. It's difficult to feel angry, anxious or blue when we're feeling grateful.

We can practise gratitude simply by feeling the emotion in our hearts; by bothering to say thank you with a message, card or letter; and by repaying a kindness. Our appreciation for people, things and experiences can also become clearer and more helpful to us when we write it down regularly, in the form of a gratitude journal.

Gratitude:

- Improves your mood and makes you feel happier.
- Helps you sleep better and more peacefully.

- ✧ Strengthens your relationships and connections.
- ✧ Builds resilience and a positive outlook.
- ✧ Is a great way to celebrate even the tiniest achievement.

Take a day to feel grateful

This is a gentle, joyful retreat day that you can play any way you choose. Begin by making a personal gratitude list of people, experiences, places and things to feel grateful for, starting small and building it up, using ideas in the box below. Then go ahead and express your gratitude for some of these, just to see how it feels, taking yourself to places that delight you during the process. End the day by turning your thanks inward, offering yourself a kind word or gesture.

> **WHO/WHAT TO FEEL GRATEFUL FOR:**
>
> **The right person at the right time:** Someone who really listened this morning. A friend who checked in just last week. A bit of advice from years back that's still guiding your next step.
>
> **Clinking glasses, shared desserts:** A meal with friends or family. A celebration that still makes you smile. Laughing until you cried. Your son or daughter's wit.
>
> **Kindness you didn't have to ask for:** Being included without asking. A stranger holding the door. Someone stepping in with exactly the right kind of help.

Quiet company, no fuss: A friendly nod from a neighbour. A hug from a child that softened your edges. Sitting with your pet, cup of tea or book in peace.

Something difficult that taught you something: An argument that gifted you patience. Feeling scared on an adventure, so you built strength. Losing a competition you were convinced you were going to win, which helped you find resilience.

Your helpers: The people who have helped you get from A to B to C in your life. The teachers, friends, parents, colleagues, anyone at all. This could include people from your past, who you haven't seen for a while.

Yourself: What in your life have you created that feels good? What qualities have helped you overcome challenges? Any exciting life events or achievements you'd like to note?

The outside that gets in: The way light fills a room. The run, cycle or walk you did yesterday. Birdsong of any kind. Swifts swooping and chasing each other outside your window. Remarkable trees. A wild place near your home.

Random things: Grapes, bikes, mountains, coffee, mojitos, music, lanterns, skinny dipping, moonstone, comedy nights, oil paintings, stars, forests. You choose. Anything goes, and there doesn't have to be a logical reason behind your choices.

Suggested schedule

On waking: Begin your gratitude list by asking yourself, who or what were you grateful for yesterday? From your breakfast smoothie to a lunchtime walk, or something supportive a friend or colleague said. Open your journal or take out some loose paper and write it down. Pick five things if you can. Then rise and nourish yourself.

Mid morning: After breakfast, settle yourself in your chosen retreat space and continue your list. Expand where your mind goes. Have fun with it. What were you grateful for last week? Last month? During this whole year? What about last year, in the last decade, since your childhood? Who and what are you grateful for in your whole life until now? Expand your gratitude list in whatever way feels right. You could write one long list, or group things into themes. Break and nourish when you need.

Mid afternoon: After a morning spent reflecting on what you're grateful for, it's time to express your gratitude. Choose one, two or three people from your list you'd like to thank, and take the time to create a genuine, heartfelt message to them. This could be digital, but, better still, why not handwrite a letter or card? You could even make a card if you feel inspired. There's something delightful about receiving something by post in today's world, when so much of our communication is online.

To enrich your experience, consider going somewhere you love, that makes you feel grateful, to write your messages, such as a beautiful local park or a favourite café. Take your time to write something that feels authentic and bespoke to the person you are thanking.

Late afternoon: When you are ready, stamp your letters and cards and go out to post them. This could be a second outing, perhaps part of a walk somewhere you like, where you can reflect on the good things in your life and the beauty that surrounds you.

For fun, and to spread love, you could also write an unstamped letter of gratitude for a stranger to find, put it in an envelope, label it 'To Whoever Finds This', and leave it somewhere public, such as in the hollow of a tree, or propped by a mirror in a bathroom.

Feel free to express your gratitude for an event, experience or something in nature too. Write down your thank yous in your journal or on loose paper, or say them in your mind or aloud.

Evening: Don't forget you. Take this evening to express gratitude for yourself. Indulge in a little bit of pampering, or make a list of all the achievements you are proud of. Close the day by writing a postcard or short note to yourself, with one brief, kind thing you'd like to remember about how fantastic you are. Plan to post it tomorrow, or tuck it somewhere where you'll find it later in your week, to uplift you.

Tips for a successful practice

- During your routines today, notice small things that bring you comfort or joy. Whether you are brushing your teeth, washing your face, making lunch, going for a walk or opening a window. There's no need to name it, just let yourself feel it.

- If you want to write a thank-you letter to someone in your past, and don't have their address, write it anyway, then put the letter aside and vow to find it out and post it at a later date.

- Remember you can be grateful for anything. As Anne Shirley says in L. M. Montgomery's novel *Anne of Green Gables*: 'I'm so glad I live in a world where there are Octobers.' What small or unexpected thing can you appreciate?

- If you are struggling to find things to feel grateful for, focus on nature – the cornflower blue of a sky, a patch of snowdrops, a gigantic oak, a cooling breeze on a hot day. Often, feeling thankfulness for non-human things can help us segue into what can sometimes be the trickier business of feeling gratitude for others.

Reflect on your practice

The morning after your retreat, see how you feel when you wake. Did expressing gratitude yesterday make you feel more hope and optimism for your life? Is there anyone or anything else you missed, that you'd still like to thank? Write it down, and vow to express your appreciation later.

Continue your practice

In the days following your retreat, use a repetitive act as a cue to mentally say thank you for something small that went right today. It could be each time you close a door, for example – your front door, car door, office door, or the fridge. This helps you choose to feel gratitude over stress or worry.

Regularly practising gratitude sharpens our awareness of the ways we're already being supported in life, often invisibly. When we recognise this, even in small ways, we build up evidence – that the world isn't out to get us, that people are mostly decent, that we're not alone, that we can afford to relax our grip a little.

So get yourself a special notebook, label it your Gratitude Journal, and each day, week or as often as you need, write down a list of people, things or experiences you are grateful for. Try for five things each time, but know that even the act of noticing one thing, in a day that has felt bleak, can make you feel more hopeful.

RETREAT FOR LONGER
PRACTISE SELF-RELIANCE

Trusting yourself keeps you centred. Less bothered about what other people might be doing or saying, and all the energy that wastes. More in tune with your own thoughts and needs. As I've heard many a Yoga teacher say, and as I now say to my own daughter as a metaphor for life: stay on your own Yoga mat. Don't glance sideways to check how far others have stretched. How gracefully they might move. That's their body, and their work. Yours is different, and more worthy of your attention.

To trust yourself is to rely on yourself. To be independent and self-sufficient. To listen to your own conscience, over the advice of others. Like going into silence (see p. 208), practising self-reliance helps us know and meet ourselves. Considering that we are essentially born alone, and that we die alone, it's pretty important too. Given the space, you'll often find that you already have the resources you need within you to take your next step.

One of the most powerful calls for independence I've read is the 1841 essay 'Self-Reliance' by pioneering transcendentalist and philosopher Ralph Waldo Emerson. His words still resonate today: 'Nothing can bring you peace but yourself,' he writes. 'To be yourself in a world that is constantly trying to make you something else is the greatest accomplishment.' Do you rely on yourself, or do you listen to the opinion of others over your own inner voice? Is it time to go your own way?

Self-reliance:

- ✧ Helps you feel more confident and able to bounce back from challenges.

- ✧ Makes it easier to make decisions that work for you.

- ✧ Helps you manage money and other resources with greater care, so you have more stability.

- Lowers stress by giving you more control over your life.
- Strengthens trust in yourself, which helps you build trust with others.
- Leads to happier relationships and a greater sense of satisfaction.

Take time out to make a field guide to your life

Take two days of focused time out to create your own field guide. This is a curated collection of words, images and light objects that appeal to you, to literally help guide you through your everyday life. In creating it, you will unfold what you have inside you, and within your life, that you can trust. You could also build your guide in stages, over a longer period of time.

Your field guide will be a book that you can keep close by or carry with you, to read and refer to, whenever you need. Creating something with care, and by yourself, like this, and looking at it consistently after, works in much the same way as affirmations (see Affirm, p. 143) or reframing our limiting beliefs (see Re-imagine your life, p. 235). It helps us to change the neuropathways in our brain, rewiring us for positive change.

To prepare your guide: Before your retreat begins, decide what you will use as your container. I use an A5 folder with sleeves in it, so I can refresh it regularly and easily carry it with me. You could work with a fresh notebook instead, and might like a larger one for more spaciousness.

Then, start to collect precious things to put in it – from your home, garden or when out and about in your daily life. What you notice says something important about what you already trust. Write or print out anything you find online in advance if you want to keep your devices off during your retreat. For some ideas, see below.

WHAT TO PUT IN YOUR FIELD GUIDE

Your own words and ideas: Your own experiences and perspectives to date offer a distinct and important wisdom, so don't forget to include what you already know.

Guiding ideas: Ideas and philosophies that resonate with you, summarised in one-liners or short paragraphs.

Resonant words: Single words, quotes, lyrics and excerpts from features, stories, poems, books, films and songs that inspire, touch or resonate with you. Print them in advance, or copy them out by hand during your retreat.

Mementos: Fragments and light objects from nature or your past that resonate with you. You may already have a stash of these buried in a drawer, or you may just start to notice things that you never did before in the run-up to your retreat.

Humour: Pictures, excerpts or notes about things you find amusing.

Dream designs: Cut-outs of ideal spaces or places you want to sit in, live in or visit, or copies of designs and patterns you find exceptional or inspiring.

Supportive faces: Photos of people who have stood the test of time and who you feel supported by, and who you in turn support and love.

> **Meaningful messages:** Print-outs of emails and messages, or handwritten cards and letters, that have touched, praised or boosted you in a meaningful way.
>
> **Role models:** Pictures of people you admire, in the public eye or who you have met along your life's path, with the qualities you admire them for written beside them.
>
> **Gratitude lists:** Lists of experiences, events, people, things in nature and objects to be grateful for so far in your life (see Choose gratitude, p. 146).

Suggested schedule

Day one: Begin and get stuck in

On waking: Begin your retreat by asking yourself, what do I believe in today? Use your journal or loose paper to write it down. Continue to ask yourself questions to tease out what you trust in life. What values are important to me? Whom do I truly love, who also supports me? Which words, pictures or ideas do I keep returning to? What truths have followed me through time? Make a note of any words or ideas that resonate with you that you want to add to your guide.

Morning: In your retreat space, choose one thing from the materials you collected before your retreat that you love the most, and make a page for it to start your field guide. Then begin choosing, cutting out, sticking in, labelling, writing, sketching and arranging everything else. Don't overthink it. Let your hands follow your instinct. Trust your own sense of what matters. Take as much time as you want. Take a break and nourish when you need.

Afternoon: After lunch, spend time collecting more things for your guide. Start by going outside, or moving slowly through your home, garden or immediate area, with one simple question in mind: 'What is trying to find its way into my field guide today?' Carry a small envelope, pouch, or piece of paper and pencil in your hand. Be curious and available to whatever calls you. It might be a feather, petal, leaf or stone. A scrap of fabric, a sliver of paper, a shape you want to sketch. A word or phrase from a book pulled from your shelf that resonates with you. A thought you have. Return to your retreat space and carry on with your guide. Take a break and nourish when you need.

Evening: After a meal, briefly review your field guide and look at what stands out. What surprises you? What feels especially clear? Then take a total break from it and do something relaxing that will help you sleep well.

Day two: Check and continue

On waking: Check in with yourself to see if there are any words, images or ideas that your subconscious has come up with for you overnight as extra fodder for your guide. Make a note of them to add to your guide later.

Morning: After breakfast, create a Me Map – a simple mind map to get to know yourself better and help build trust in your choices. Draw a circle in the middle of a fresh page and write your name inside. From there, add branches for whatever feels true for you with quick, honest notes about yourself. You could note your social disposition (introvert, extrovert, bit of both); energy patterns (vibrant in the morning, come alive in the evening); flow activities (what you love doing so much that you lose track of time, see p. 100); stress triggers, strengths, challenges and so on. This is just for you, and there are no wrong answers. Add it to your guide if you want to.

Mid morning to mid afternoon: Enjoy hunting for fresh inspiration for your guide. Explore your local bookshop, take yourself on a walk, people watch. A gallery or museum could spark a connection, and you might bring home a postcard of a piece that moved you. Visit a charity shop or antiques market, and choose something small that catches your eye. Or simply sit in a café and note a phrase from a conversation or from your own reflections in your notebook.

Late afternoon: Return to building your guide, taking a break when you need. You may find yourself refining with more clarity now. Carry on until you feel you have 'finished' it, leaving a few blank pages you can add to at a later date.

Evening: Sit a while with what you've made. Read it like a text written in your own private language. Let it reflect something back to you about what you trust today, what you want to let go of, and what you now need. Then do something frivolous to relax before you sleep.

Tips for a successful practice

- Feel free to choose a different title for your guide that feels personal to you. Your book of truths? Your personal canon? I call mine 'My Simplicity Book' (see p. 158).

- Allow your guide to be unfiltered and honest. You're making something only you could make. Let it be imperfect. You don't have to work from front to back in your guide – be drawn to whatever place you want things to go.

- If you gather objects, be sure they are light and small, so you can carry your guide around with you as you need. Even the simplest object – a ticket stub, a pressed flower, or a scrap of paper with your own words on it – can become a memento that resonates.

✦ Don't allow yourself to be swayed or influenced by family or friends this weekend. This is your field guide, and no one else's. Be like Madam Westover, the grounded matriarch in Helen Hull's novel *Heat Lightning*, who: 'had so much in herself, she had no need to walk around in the lives of others, interfering.'

MY SIMPLICITY BOOK

I call my own field guide 'My Simplicity Book', and I regularly edit and change it. At the time of writing, it opens with a line from an upbeat boat driver named Alvin, who once said to me during a torrential downpour, 'that ain't rain, that's just liquid sunshine,' as he steered us across a relentlessly choppy sea. It moves on to a gratitude list of other life events I've loved the most, and a note of my current values (harmony, beauty, stability, etc.).

On other pages, there's a pen-and-ink drawing of a swimmer, with a shell from my local beach taped beside it. Above it, the words 'keep yourself rare' – a suggestion I love. Scattered throughout are other dictums I've come across, such as 'no news, no shoes', which is written beside a strip of cotton from a treasured kaftan I wore until it fell apart.

I have a colourful postcard of David Hockney's treehouse, which speaks to me of charm and safety. A photo of a home office on Rhodes with a sea view that inspires me (see Declutter your stuff, p. 58). At the core are photos of family and friends I love and feel loved by, and messages and cards that have boosted me when I've felt stuck.

> I have a few pictures of talented people I admire, with a quality I admire them for written beside them (such as Maggie Smith – witty; Andrew Scott – sexy; Wes Anderson – unconventional; Rachel Cusk – honest; Barack Obama – humane).
>
> In the final pages, a piece of sea-worn ceramic I found at a liberating time of my life. A copy of Alice Walker's strangely comforting poem 'Expect Nothing'. A black-and-white photo of my late grandmother, Minny, on a motorbike. It's part collage, part memento, and it helps me trust myself and the good stuff of life I've found, especially when things are feeling wobbly.

Reflect on your practice

On waking the morning after your retreat, note how you feel and what you are thinking about. Is there anything you trust more now than you did before you started? Place your guide somewhere you'll see it over the following week, and let it keep speaking to you as the noise of your life returns.

Continue your practice

Add to or change your field guide throughout the year, or create a brand new one at a future date when you feel this one has served its purpose. You could also create a 'self-trust jar' and keep it in a favourite room of your home. Each time something strikes you as true, write it on a piece of paper, fold it up and put it into the jar. When your sense of independence is tested, pick a piece of paper from the jar to boost your confidence. Jars such as this are also a way to add surprise and delight to any future self-devised retreats you do (see Retreat Toolkit, p. 15).

Hosted retreats to foster self-trust

Hosted retreats of all kinds, from Yoga and Meditation to creative and coaching retreats, can help rebuild self-trust – not by offering answers, but by creating the conditions where people can hear themselves think. With fewer decisions to make and no pressure to perform, the background noise of daily life fades. What's left is the chance to notice what you really want or need, both in the moment and in your life. A good retreat host doesn't direct the process – they shape the environment that makes it possible.

This effect is even stronger on a private, solo retreat, or in a group where no one knows you. Without the weight of familiar roles, you're free to meet yourself just as you are. Every small choice, from skipping a session for a lie-in, to only eating when you're hungry, becomes quiet proof that you can listen to yourself and trust what you hear. With time to reflect, without rush or pressure for breakthroughs, you get the rare chance to see yourself clearly.

RECLAIM

'Oh life, why must you always leave so little time to live?'
Adelaide Love

What do you need back in your life that you have been missing? If you feel pushed and pulled in all directions, washed out but wired, it might be time to work out some strategies to reclaim yourself.

Reclaim means 'to take back something that was yours'. In the context of retreating, this is not the tax you have overpaid, or the suitcase that's been lost in transit, but the time, energy, space, self-respect and other aspects of your life you may have squandered – or that others have been all too happy to squander for you.

In our constantly connected world, having time or energy can feel far more luxurious than being able to stay somewhere gorgeous. Creating daily space for deep rest, learning how to set boundaries that work for you, and spending proper time away from screens, can refresh us entirely, so we can deal with the changes and relish the joys we are sure to find ahead.

How much time do you have to retreat?

- ✦ An hour – De-excite (p. 163)
- ✦ A day – Say no (p. 169)
- ✦ Longer – Unplug (p. 177)

Whatever you choose, refer to the Retreat Toolkit (p. 15) to help you prepare for each retreat.

Start with a check-in

Write in your journal or think to yourself:

- ✦ *I need more time/space/energy/something else in my life so that I can . . .*
- ✦ *The last time I did something I didn't want to do was . . .*
- ✦ *When I think of my smartphone, I feel . . .*

RETREAT FOR AN HOUR
DE-EXCITE

How do you de-excite yourself on a daily basis? I first heard this intriguing word when I learned the mantra-based technique of Vedic Meditation, on a retreat with Jillian Lavender, co-founder of the London and New York Meditation Centres. In the context of retreating, to de-excite means to properly rest during a busy day, so you have the time and energy you need to continue to make the most of things – in a smoother, calmer and kinder frame of mind.

'The antidote to stress is deep rest – it's that simple,' says Jillian. Yet most of us just carry on wading through treacle, until we hit the reward of a stiff drink or a hot bath at the end of a stressful day. Pressing pause instead, and truly stopping before we are broken, actually creates more time and energy for us. It helps us to engage fully with what comes after. To catch up on sleep if we've had a disturbed night. Deal better with, and recover more quickly from, stressful situations. Respond, rather than react, to challenging people or emails.

Vedic Meditation needs to be learned in person from an experienced teacher, who can guide you through the process and give you the correct mantra. As an introduction to what it feels like to de-excite your body and mind, take an hour to tune out the world, tune into your body and get a taste of what regular de-excitement might feel like.

A PAUSE FOR VEDIC MEDITATION

Vedic Meditation is a mantra-based technique from the Veda, the ancient body of knowledge from India that also gave rise to Yoga (see Embody, p. 119) and

Ayurveda (see Refresh yourself, p. 51). Passed down from teacher to student by the people of the Indus Valley for generations, it was brought to the West in the late 1950s by Maharishi Mahesh Yogi, who famously later taught it to The Beatles during their stay at his ashram in Rishikesh.

To practise, you simply sit, close your eyes and gently repeat a mantra silently in the mind, without effort or control. *Mantra* in Sanskrit means 'instrument for the mind', and it's a simple, resonant sound, with no meaning, given in person by a teacher. The mantra's charm, rather than your willpower, draws the mind inward, until it becomes more subtle, then disappears, leaving the mind quiet and the body in a de-excited state.

In this state, the body produces neuro-hormones, such as serotonin, that counteract the chemistry of stress – whether that's felt as sadness, fear or anger. Thoughts that arise are simply signs of stress release, not obstacles, and with regular practice, longer-held tensions also begin to dissolve.

As Jillian Lavender explains in her book *Why Meditate*? the mantra in Vedic Meditation is not a concentration tool like the breath, but an orientating device, that draws the mind towards a supremely restful state of consciousness. Unlike breath-based practices, such as Vipassana Meditation, which hold attention at the level of thought, Vedic Meditation settles the mind into being, allowing the body to experience a depth of physiological rest that research shows can surpass sleep.

Over time, we release stress more quickly than we accumulate it, experiencing greater clarity, resilience and ease. Meditation also becomes a lesson in letting go of control: as Lavender points out, change is the only constant, and while resisting it is depleting, adapting to it is the very essence of evolution.

I learned the technique in just two hours a day over four days. It's the only Meditation method I have managed to bring back from a retreat into my daily life, and a twice-daily 20-minute dose of it has been my daily reset for many years now. It's effortless, and you can do it anywhere you can sit comfortably and safely close your eyes, from graveyards and restaurant loos to benches in galleries, on the sofas in shops, in cars and on trains.

De-exciting can help us:

- ✦ Feel ready for our day ahead and re-energised for our evenings.

- ✦ Rest deeply, sleep better and release stress to prevent ill health.

- ✦ Think more clearly and manage our emotions more effectively.

- ✦ Accept and deal well with change, and approach life more creatively.

- ✦ Connect better with family and friends, and show up more fully in our lives.

Meditation also allows the 'small self' to recognise its connection to something greater – an ocean of consciousness that links us all. With regular practice, this expanded sense of awareness deepens and grows.

Take an hour to tune into your body

Settle somewhere comfortable, on a chair or cushion, in whatever position you choose, but with your back supported. You do not have to be cross-legged – just sit however you like. Have an analogue clock close by, or your phone on airplane mode with the clock showing. To check the time at any point, feel free to open your eyes and glance at your clock, then gently close them again.

Notice: Take a moment to notice your body. Identify the place that feels the most tense, and gently allow your attention to rest there. At first the tension might amplify, but after a little while, just by focusing on it, it will start to dissolve. Be patient. When you are ready, after a minute or two, move to the next place you feel tension, and so on. You might move from tight shoulders following too much computer work, to a sore knee from yesterday's run, to a cut on your arm, to an ache in your temples. Gently follow your aches and pains for 20 minutes or so.

Rest: When you have finished scanning the tensions in your body, keep your eyes gently closed and allow your thoughts to come and go. If you feel like it, shift your position or lie down. Cover yourself with a blanket or a shawl. Your mind will have started to settle naturally during your practice. Let it continue to settle. Rest for 20 minutes or so.

Resist: Don't try to control anything or stop your thinking – it will be impossible. Just let your awareness rest where it wants to, and you will naturally settle down.

Return: When you feel ready, open your eyes slowly. Allow yourself to enjoy this restful state. Take your time, enjoying simply being, for the rest of your hour. Take a moment to notice how you feel, then stand up and stretch gently. Sip from a glass of water, before moving on with your day.

Tips for a successful practice

- ✧ The only thing you can do wrong when you practise Meditation is to 'try'. So don't try, or force anything, during this hour of de-excitement.

- ✧ Let your breathing be natural and easy throughout your hour.

- ✧ The timings suggested are only rough. Go with what feels right to you.

Reflect on your practice

How did you feel after your session? Did you feel quieter and more at ease? Do you need more of it? During the week that follows, first thing in the morning on waking, or late in your afternoon or early evening when you feel tired, just sit quietly with your eyes closed for a few moments and tap into how your body feels. You'll be starting to make space for a regular practice.

Continue your practice

Many people say they're too busy to meditate regularly, but Meditation actually creates time by resetting you, helping you become more focused and efficient. Apps, podcasts and online courses can introduce you to various Meditation techniques, and, often, finding the time to meditate simply means choosing to set aside distractions or inconsequential tasks, such as endless scrolling on social media, or obsessing over admin that can wait.

If de-exciting your body and mind on a regular basis works for you, take time to find a professional near you who teaches Vedic Meditation in person with care and integrity (see Resources, p. 261). Once you have learned, hosted Rounding Retreats are open to you at gorgeous places around the world. 'Rounding' is a practice of repeating one-hour cycles that include gentle *asanas*, simple *pranayama*, Meditation and rest. It's what Prudence in The Beatles' song 'Dear Prudence' is doing, which is why she can't 'come out to play'.

RETREAT FOR A DAY

SAY NO

I've spent too much of my life doing things that I don't really want to because I feel I obligated. What about you? Saying yes to a tempting invite when your whole body is screaming 'put me to bed'. Taking on extra work for the money when it would have been better to have the spare time. Looking at social media of every single kind until eventually you might, as I did, listen to the palpitations of your heart and take yourself off all of it. The blissful relief!

How much of your life have you spent so far doing things you didn't want to? Imagine how much time, space, money and energy you could reclaim if you felt better equipped to say no with conviction and grace. We say yes to things we don't really want to do for many reasons. We feel that we 'should', we don't want to offend, or we fear missing out. We want to fit in, be liked and avoid seeming lazy or uncooperative. Sometimes, fear, shame or guilt push us to people-please for approval. Or we agree to help someone we barely know, hoping they'll like us more.

Starting-over coach and retreat leader Kate Emmerson first inspired me to truly say no to what was not working for me on a writer's retreat, when I was trying to find more time to write. 'Saying yes when you mean no can lead to situations that truly drain you,' she explains. 'It signals that your time and energy are endless, that your wellbeing doesn't matter.' Overcommitting can strain relationships, leading to last-minute cancellations and disappointment. Whereas saying no when we mean it is authentic, helping us to attract the right people and life for ourselves.

Saying no:

- Is a brave act of self-respect.
- Sets boundaries and helps us live with integrity.
- Teaches others how to treat you, and to treat themselves, better.
- Fosters healthier relationships.
- Makes space for what truly matters.
- Can even save us money.

Take a day to prepare to say no

On this retreat day, you can relish setting new boundaries for yourself. You'll start by making a list of things you want to say no to, using the ideas below as a guide. You'll then build on your list before practising saying no, to see how it feels.

Have courage – even embarking on this retreat day is an act of saying 'no'. By blocking off time for yourself, you've already begun reclaiming your life. It's worth pausing to congratulate yourself for that.

Note that if you want to refer to your calendar and it's online, it's best to turn your notifications off before you use it, so you can stay digitally switched off and focused on the tasks at hand.

Things you could say no to

Invitations: For regular social gatherings such as a lunch, dinner, party, gig or evening drinks, or for one-off events such as a work conference, wedding, funeral, festival, weekend away, group holiday and so on.

Requests from others: An extra task a colleague has given you, or a favour a friend or family member has asked of you.

Memberships: For gyms, societies or streaming services. Cancelling those you feel bound by, but that don't serve you, can be liberating and save you money too.

Appointment times: Can you cancel a haircut or other appointment you don't really need, to free up space?

Regular commitments: Such as clubs, committees, classes or voluntary work.

Future commitments: We often say that we'll do something at a future date, instead of now, thinking that that's when we'll have more time. But, actually, the time you have available now will probably be the same in a few months or even years, unless you are about to substantially change your lifestyle. Be wary of over-committing, even if it feels a long way off.

Your to do list: Is there something on your to do list that's been on there just a little bit too long? Be honest with yourself – if you're never going to do it, cross it off. It's just another layer of stress you see every time you look at your list. Do you really need it done?

Digital demands: When and if to look at, and how to respond to, social media, messages and emails.

Phone calls: Schedule in calls you want and need, and switch your phone on silent or off for the rest of the time.

Work meetings: How many of these do you really need to attend, on or offline? Can you save time for yourself, and your colleagues, by suggesting you have fewer as a team?

Interruptions: Make your own version of a 'do not disturb' sign – failing that, say you're not at home.

Staying in the loop: You don't have to be on top of local and international news – it's okay to say 'I don't know' or even 'I'm not interested'.

Having an opinion: That person who always wants you to join in a political discussion? Perhaps you don't want to this time. And that's okay.

Pretending: When we act against what we really want to do, we are masking ourselves. Why pretend to be someone we are not? Life is too short.

Participating: In our societies, we often feel obliged to participate in whatever everyone else is doing. But we don't have to. It can take us years to fully realise this.

Following the crowd: Wherever and whoever you are, protect your boundaries and be your own judge (see Practise self-reliance, see p. 152).

Suggested schedule

On waking: Open your journal or take some loose paper and begin your list of things you want to say no to. Start by asking yourself, who or what in your life right now do you most obviously, in your gut, want to say no to? It could be a one-off situation, or an ongoing commitment. Would you rather stay in and have a hot bath than go out drinking this Friday? Has your time on the school committee come to an end? Jot down three easy wins.

Morning: After breakfast, take a look at your calendar for the next month or so. Ask yourself, how do the events you have in there make you feel? Then take yourself outside for a short walk, bike or cycle in the fresh air, to give your subconscious time to work on things.

On your return, settle yourself in your chosen retreat space and return to your 'say no' list. Build on it by delving deeper.

What else do you want to say no to? Start with tomorrow, then move on to the rest of your week, the rest of the month, and your wider year ahead. Refer to your calendar as you need. Come up with at least ten things, up to as many things as you like. See the ideas on p. 170 as prompts.

If it's useful, jot down your personal reasons beside each thing you want to say no to. Clear reminders make it easier to stand firm. For example, if you don't drink, you might note how drained you feel at the pub when surrounded by drunk people who keep repeating themselves, which can help you decline invites and avoid over-committing.

Afternoon: After lunch, when you have a list with which you are reasonably satisfied, choose one, two or three things you would like to say no to today. Make them easy wins. Whether that's cancelling an appointment, drafting an email to send when you're back online, or popping a note in your calendar to cancel something bigger when you have more time. Practise taking action now, and it will be easier to say no to the other things on your list as you get the hang of it. For how to do this, see Helpful ways of saying no, below.

Evening: Rest, have your meal, share your feelings with a friend or enjoy time alone relaxing as you choose. Celebrate the fact that you have begun to reclaim some time and energy. Before sleep, briefly refer back to your list, and add or tweak anything that has come to you.

HELPFUL WAYS OF SAYING NO

Take your time: Crafting a kind decline takes effort, but it saves time in the long run. If needed, buy time with 'Can I get back to you soon?'

Be gracious: Say no with kindness. You don't need to over-explain, but avoid abruptness to prevent hurt feelings.

Suggest alternatives: A softened 'no' can include another option: 'I can join, but just for an hour' or 'I think Victoria has more time right now'.

Delay your yes: No can be temporary: 'I'd love to, but can we plan it a few weeks later?'

Trust others: Honest declines can encourage others to be more authentic. A splash of humour never goes amiss too: 'I need my downtime just to lie down in a dark room!'

No need to justify: A simple, polite decline often works: 'Thanks for thinking of me, but I can't make it. Hope it goes brilliantly!'

Speak in person: Sometimes, a phone call or face-to-face chat makes things kinder and clearer.

Practise: Start small to build confidence for trickier situations.

Tips for a successful practice

- ✧ Allow discomfort. Saying no can feel awkward, and it may disappoint others. But if it's the right decision for you, it's worth it. Practise tolerating discomfort, and your anxiety around saying no will ease over time.

- ✧ Have courage. Dare to go against the crowd – you might find that others don't want to do something either. Our FOMO, or fear of missing out, can feel particularly strong if we are on social media. But trust that what you need will find you.

- ✧ Choose wisely. For big events like weddings or festivals, take time to decide. Go if it truly matters to you or to someone you love. Find the right balance. If you feel stuck, take some time to connect with your thoughts and feelings by journalling (see Journal, p. 69), or sit quietly and tune into your body (see De-excite, p. 163).

- Be your own judge. Don't let imagined opinions dictate your choices. Trust that you are enough just as you are, whether you're spending time with family, exercising, or simply resting.

- Trust your intuition. Before committing, check in with yourself. Does it feel right? If the thought of it makes you tired, resentful or uneasy, use that as a sign to say no.

- Own your choices. For years, I'd say I was 'working' when, really, I was going for a walk, having a swim or getting a massage, thinking it was more acceptable. Now, I own my self-care, and in doing so, my friends tell me I often encourage others to do the same.

- Embrace what you say yes to. When you do commit, follow through – last-minute cancellations create ill will. And when you can't say no, lean into it. If my daughter needs to talk late at night, I make tea, wrap myself in a shawl and listen, knowing that while I may lose sleep, I'll be fed by my connection with her.

Reflect on your practice

During the days following your retreat, check in with how you feel about saying no. Do you feel guilty, or sad, or liberated, or something else? Ask yourself why. Know that there is no right or wrong way to feel. If you feel inspired, continue to work through the list you have made, and aim to say no to one thing each day until it is cleared. Take a moment each time, to check in with how it feels, before and after, so you learn to trust your intuition more.

Continue your practice

Feel free to add more things to your 'say no' list during the following weeks, and pledge to always keep a 'say no' list in your journal. Whenever you feel overwhelmed in life, take some time out to review your commitments. Check your calendar – what can you say no to today, this week, or this month?

Regularly doing this will help you free up time, space, money and energy, making it easier to manage overcommitment year-round and say a great big YES to all the stuff that makes your heart sing. I find it useful to recite psychotherapist Fiona Arrigo's cleverly simple phrase when I'm feeling wobbly: 'Know your no'.

Saying no might not often be easy, but it is a gift. Done with kindness, as an act of self-respect, it can help us and others live with more integrity and stay balanced. The slight melancholy I sometimes feel when I turn down a social event, even though I know it's what I need, inspired my poem 'Small Group Gathering' (see p. 272).

RETREAT FOR LONGER

UNPLUG

When was the last time you used a digital device? Chances are it was only a few minutes, even seconds, ago. Technology is incredible on many levels, but our constant connectivity drains and demotivates us, and regular unplugging is essential to our wellbeing. It not only gives us the chance for deep rest, but it helps us manage our digital media as tools, and change our relationship with them, rather than allowing them to be tyrants that manage us, so that we have our attention and focus back for what matters in life.

I took myself off all personal social media years ago, mainly because I felt agitated and curiously lonely using it. I also found myself scrolling, only to look up and realise the sun had already moved across half the sky and that I had missed my opportunity to get out for a walk in the early morning light I like. What about you? Your tolerance levels might be higher than mine, but you'll know you're ready to unplug when your digital use leaves you grumpy, anxious, stressed out, isolated, distracted or exhausted. Young people are especially vulnerable to the harmful effects of online media.

Without the natural stopping points we used to have – when we had to wait a week for the next episode of a favourite TV series, for example – we can tirelessly scroll, binge and refresh, hooked by hits of dopamine, the neurotransmitter that fuels our brain's reward system. As Dr Anna Lembke explains in her book *Dopamine Nation*, dopamine reinforces pleasurable behaviours, but overstimulation can lower its baseline and desensitise us.

This means we need stronger stimuli – more tech use – to feel the same pleasure. Which is what makes it addictive, not just for joy, but also for outrage or frustration. Endless notifications and online distractions keep us in a state of partial attention, reducing our focus and increasing our stress. A digital detox helps reset this cycle.

Taking time out from tech:

- Restores our control over our time and attention.
- Boosts our energy and mental clarity.
- Rests our overstimulated brains.
- Sparks creativity.
- Reshapes our relationship with digital tools and devices.
- Rekindles face-to-face connections.
- Helps us feel less stressed and lonely.

Take time out for a digital detox

Unplugging your devices for the duration of *any* retreat is recommended. But if you are particularly frazzled, or find it difficult to switch off, taking dedicated time out to do this with intention can be liberating, relaxing, and empower us with the awareness we need to manage our device use more effectively in everyday life.

You could start with a few days, and build up to a longer digital detox at a later date. Choose any two consecutive days you know you can handle being offline, and make your detox last from the evening before your first day to the morning after your second. Follow the guidelines below, then relax into your personalised schedule, going with your flow and energy as your retreat progresses.

Before your retreat: Assess how you usually use your devices, and plan simple alternatives. Need a clock? Use an analogue one. Want music, podcasts or guided meditations? Play records,

CDs, or offline downloads. Keep things simple – this retreat is about paring back. See Digital resistance, p. 37, for more tips on staying offline.

Decide what activities you'd like to do (see p. 180 for ideas). Prioritise the ones that make you feel good, sharing them with device-free family members or friends if you so choose. Keep plans low-key and stress-free. This isn't the time for big challenges.

During your retreat: Rather than reaching for your phone, reach for your journal or loose paper when you feel the need for tech. Write the message you want to send, the list you need to make, the thing you want to delete, the account you want to check, and so on. This will be a useful resource to look back on after your time out.

Your notes might read: 'Saturday morning: Really missing Instagram', 'Saturday afternoon: I wonder how Ellis is doing in France? Frustrated I can't just instantly message him', 'Saturday evening: I feel anxious that I can't see my emails, but lighter too', 'So bored – I realise how reliant I am on Netflix to entertain me'. And so on.

On your last afternoon: Start to get clarity on what you do – and do not – need and want from your electronic devices when you switch things back on, and make an action list in your journal or on loose paper. Ask yourself: Which practical apps and other digital tools truly benefit my personal life and work, and which don't? What can I simply let go of? What tools at work would I like to review with colleagues on my return? Are there any social media accounts or messaging groups I have that don't make me feel good? Can I delete any?

On your last morning: Act on your list. Take yourself out of messaging groups you no longer need access to. Check and increase your privacy settings. Tidy up your social media accounts. For favourite platforms you want to keep, choose which irritating or upsetting accounts you can mute, snooze or unfollow. This way, you won't see posts that drain you, but you also avoid creating drama by unfollowing or blocking someone. For apps you can't quite let go of, hide them, or use your phone's settings to limit your access, so you're less tempted to use them out of habit. Somewhat strangely, there is also an app that helps you block your use of apps!

Things to do without your digital devices

EXPLORE

- Plan a day-long countryside hike or bike ride with a picnic, and take a friend who is happy to leave their phone at home. Or take yourself off for a more vigorous adventure (see Find your flow, p. 100).

- Immerse yourself in culture, history or art at a museum, gallery, historic house or landmark, or take a camera or sketchbook out and look for beauty in unexpected places – the light on a derelict wooden door, an intricate spider's web, astonishing wall art (see Be an artist, p. 108).

- Potter around a craft, antique or farmers market for unexpected finds, homemade treats, local charm and the buzz of a lively place.

CONNECT

- Host a meal or a low-key board games night with family or friends who are happy to leave their phones at home, or play a game of tennis, badminton or another sport you enjoy with a friend.

- Book ahead to see something live such as a gig, play or comedy show, leaving your phone at home.

- Write a meaningful letter or postcard to a friend, a family member, or even your future self, or spend time with animals or your pet.

MAKE AND DO

- Take photos with a disposable, polaroid or film camera, get crafty in other ways (see Find your flow, p. 100), garden (see Garden p. 74) or do something creative in your home (see Be an artist, p. 108).

- Rediscover something you once loved. Pick up an instrument, throw a ball against a wall, tackle a puzzle, jigsaw or crossword.

JUST RELAX

- Try breathwork exercises (see Breathe, p. 191), move gently or listen to music (see Embody p. 119), or indulge yourself (see Treat yourself, p. 126).

- Simply spend time outside – feel the air, watch the clouds, touch the grass, listen to birdsong, watch the sunrise or stargaze away from bright lights.

- Read a book you can lose yourself in (see A Pause For Reading, p. 29).

Suggested schedule

The evening before your retreat: Finish up all emails and messages in good time, so you feel comfortable turning off all your devices. Put them away out of sight in a cupboard or drawer, preferably in a room you are unlikely to visit. If you can't trust yourself, give them to a family member, neighbour or friend to look after. Make a pledge not to revisit them until the morning after your digital detox. Take a few minutes to clear and tidy your space, creating an inviting and calm environment. Aim for a relaxing night's sleep to help you start the detox refreshed.

Day one: Disengage and discover

Morning: On waking, thank yourself for the fact that you don't have to turn your phone on today, or look at a screen of any kind. You might meditate or tune in to your body (see De-excite, p. 163), then journal to tune in to how you feel before a refreshing shower, some morning movement and breakfast.

Daytime: You could choose to visit a local museum, gallery or historic house, and take your time exploring and absorbing the atmosphere without rush. Or take yourself off for a solo adventure doing a sport you love. For lunch, you could eat at a favourite quiet spot to savour the moment, sharing it with a friend who's also without their phone if you choose. An afternoon stroll through a nearby craft or farmers market might offer delightful discoveries.

Evening: Perhaps host a relaxed gathering over a meal with family or friends who are also unplugging, or go out with someone you love to a comedy night or gig, leaving your phone at home. Enjoy the pleasure of being sociable without digital distractions. Share stories, laughter or music before an earlyish night.

Day two: Relax and review

Morning: You could begin your day by stepping outside for a nature walk, noticing the textures, sounds and smells around you. Enjoy a nourishing breakfast that grounds you. Then take some time to journal about any insights or revelations you've had about your digital use so far.

Daytime: Meet a friend for a scenic hike or bike ride on a coastal or country trail. Take a picnic along and enjoy the natural surroundings and good company away from screens. You could dip in the sea or a local river after if you feel like it.

Late afternoon to early evening: On your return, open your journal and start to get clarity about what you do and do not want from your digital devices once you switch things back on. Turn this into an action list for tomorrow morning (see On your last afternoon, p. 179).

Evening: Congratulate yourself for having spent two full days without your devices. Perhaps soak in a long hot bath, sketch or read by a fire, or massage your feet or head to unwind before lights out.

The morning after your retreat: Allow yourself a slow start to your day. Wake naturally, and move, dress and nourish yourself before switching on any devices. When you are ready, mindfully turn on your phone, keeping your notifications off. Enjoy a hot cup of your favourite brew while you follow through on your action list. Act now, while you feel refreshed and motivated to take care of yourself. You can carry on this process over the coming week if you would like more time. Then move slowly into the rest of your day. Alternatively – just carry on digitally detoxing!

Tips for a successful practice

- ✧ Pledge to yourself that you will avoid all screens for your digital detox – this includes TV, radio and the cinema as well as your phone, laptop, tablet, Kindle and any other devices. You'll need to be off work, and away from work calls. Avoid things that might entice you to break your detox too, including a friend who cannot get off their phone, and drugs or alcohol.

- ✧ Make this a few days of joy, away from the daily grind. Avoid dealing with any stressful situations, whether that's boring life admin, fixing a broken appliance or sorting out a work issue. Reward yourself with whatever serves you, whether that's nutritious treats, a massage or something more ambitious.

- Allow yourself to be with your feelings. Feel free to feel as angry and angsty as you want. You may well be bored. Sit with it – you'll slowly build up a tolerance to it. If being away from your devices is annoying you, let yourself be annoyed. Ask yourself why you are feeling these things. Know the time will pass.

- You might find that you gain clarity on life situations whilst you are away from your devices. If something comes up, make a note of what you will do after your weekend, from the small to the serious. Your notes might read: 'Decided I need to add Reformer Pilates to my routine to get stronger. Maybe this is something I can do with Ned?' Or 'My friendship with Ira is exhausting. How can I press pause gently on it for a while?' And so on.

- Don't stress if you don't get through all your action list on your last morning – pledge to carry on during your spare time over the following few days while you're still motivated.

Reflect on your practice

The day after your digital detox ends, reflect on the experience while it is still fresh in your mind. Look back at any notes you made during your retreat, and digest how being without your devices has affected you, for good or ill. How did you feel going out without your phone – untethered, liberated, anxious? Why was that? Which devices or apps did you genuinely miss or struggle without, and which do you only use out of habit? Continue to reflect each evening for as long as it serves you.

Continue your practice

We don't have to look at a digital detox as a total rejection of technology, but as a valuable opportunity to rediscover our attention and shape new habits for a more intentional, fulfilling life. Gradually reintroducing technology, in deliberate, mindful ways that work for you, can have a massive positive impact on daily life.

To manage your tech use ongoing:

Go analogue: Arguably, as we rely more on tech, we also become increasingly unable to get off it or use anything else. If this bothers you, look for ways of using offline things instead of digital on an ongoing basis. A notebook rather than the notes on your phone. A paper diary rather than your online calendar for significant events. Reading a physical book instead of using a Kindle or scrolling through articles on your device. A mechanical clock, a film camera, a CD player or vinyl records, a music player to play downloaded, offline tracks. Chances are, the more you're off your tech, the more you'll want to be.

Choose your commitments: Know that you don't have to be part of everything. One of the most freeing parts of a digital detox is realising you can say no to more online courses, meetings and events. Support what truly matters and ignore the rest (see Say no, p. 169).

Unplug daily: Develop your own set of phone-free rituals, so you can unplug easily on a daily basis. Switch your phone on later at a set time. Entice your household to agree to not having phones at meal times. Go for phone-free walks. Mute notifications and set fixed times to check emails, apps and social feeds. Limit checking news or group chats to once a day or less. Keep your phone on silent except when you are expecting a call. Reply to messages quickly, or wait until you can respond fully. Use screen-time settings to keep limits in place. Keep your phone out of reach for part of the day. In the evening, switch it off, store it in another room and avoid charging it by your bed.

Consider something radical: Is there something radical you would like to do to bring more silence and calm into your life? Delete an app you've relied on for a long time, take yourself off all social media, actively resist using AI, get rid of your smartphone altogether? Take some time to decide what will work for you.

Lean on your community: Ask trusted friends to keep you in the loop about anything important you might miss, especially if you step away from social platforms. Trust that what matters will find its way to you.

Make it a habit: Once you experience what it feels like to have a total break from your devices, you can use that as a stepping-stone for a longer digital detox, so you have healthier habits for the rest of your month, year and even life. Introduce a regular digital detox day or weekend into every month, or make it longer. Ask your friends and family to join you. You will hopefully, like me, find a freedom in taking yourself off your electronic devices regularly. I know when it's time to get offline when I fantasise about it, a feeling that inspired my poem 'I am on a Zoom call' (see p. 274).

Hosted digital detox retreats

Immersive digital detox retreats around the world can help you switch off all your devices, deeply rest and understand better how to manage them on your return to everyday life. Rather than requiring you to rely on weak wifi signals or self-control, they give you the option of removing your devices and keeping them safely away from you.

Options range from luxury wellbeing programmes with digital detox butlers who keep guests' devices safe for them, to off-grid cabins designed for complete disconnection, to simpler tech-light stays in countryside locations where wifi and screens are intentionally absent.

Switching off devices is an easy way to bring quiet and inward connection into retreats of any kind, and many general retreats, from mindfulness breaks to walking and Yoga holidays, will actively encourage it with a wifi-free policy, or dedicated areas and times where you can check messages if you need to.

SETTLE

*'Take refuge in your senses, open up
To all the small miracles you rushed through'*

John O'Donohue
from the blessing 'For One Who is Exhausted'

What do we mean by settle? To settle is to find a place of stillness that works for you. You might settle down, settle your differences, settle a bill or a debt, settle a blanket over your shoulders or those of someone you love. Settling is a way of resolving things. An act of grounding, and the creation of a secure base.

To settle ourselves can be one of the hardest things to do. To stop holding our breath, and breathe freely and deeply. To be present, so we can concentrate. To give ourselves time in silence, so we can listen to what we might already know. To simply be still, while the world around us is constantly moving.

I feel to settle is to give up striving or trying to fix something, and instead quietly return to what's already inside us. If we find tools to calm our minds and bodies, we can use them to access that calm whenever we need, whether through deep breathing, mindful attention or quiet moments alone.

How much time do you have to retreat?

- An hour – Breathe (p. 191)
- A day – Be mindful (p. 199)
- Longer – Go into silence (p. 208)

Whatever you choose, refer to the Retreat Toolkit (p. 15) to help you prepare for each retreat.

Start with a check-in

Write in your journal or think to yourself:

- *At this moment, I am/am not holding my breath . . . I think this is because . . .*
- *Right now I can smell, taste, touch, hear and see . . .*
- *The thought of not talking makes me feel . . .*

RETREAT FOR AN HOUR

BREATHE

Do you sometimes catch yourself holding your breath? When you're hanging out washing, caught in a traffic jam, or waiting for news that will affect your family, perhaps? How do you physically feel when this happens? Are your shoulders up at ear level, your chest tight, or your jaw clenched? Next time you are aware of this, take a huge, deep breath, drop your shoulders, and reapproach the task at hand with slightly more ease.

Breath has long been seen as more than just air. Across civilisations, it has been revered as a tool for regulation, resilience and release (see A Pause For Our Breath as a Bridge, p. 192). Though we breathe instinctively every moment of the day, breathing consciously is a powerful, free tool we can use to support for our health and wellbeing.

Simply slowing down and deepening our rate of breathing activates our parasympathetic nervous system (see Embody, p. 119). It helps release built-up stress and guides us into ease, both in daily chaos and during difficult moments. Taken further, therapeutic breathwork with a trained therapist can also release long-held stress and trauma, radically transforming our wellbeing.

A regular breathwork practice:

- ✧ Reduces our stress levels and regulates our emotions.
- ✧ Increases our energy by enhancing oxygen uptake.
- ✧ Boosts circulation by increasing blood flow.
- ✧ Expands lung capacity by strengthening our breathing muscles.

- ✧ Helps improve immunity by supporting the body's natural healing response.
- ✧ Expands our awareness of ourselves and our lives.

A PAUSE FOR OUR BREATH AS A BRIDGE

Across civilisations and cultures, the simple act of breathing has been used as a bridge to link mind and body, the spiritual and the everyday. Modern breathwork is rooted in and enriched by this universal wisdom, inviting us to follow the world's heritage and take a long, deep breath.

In ancient Egypt, for example, burial texts like the Books of Breathing were placed in tombs to ensure the dead could breathe, speak and thrive in the afterlife, while rituals such as the Opening of the Mouth ceremony symbolically restored breath to the soul.

Pranayama (yogic breathwork) has been practised for thousands of years to balance body and mind and expand consciousness (see A Pause for Yoga, p. 122), while in Buddhist traditions, mindful breathing is central to cultivating calm and insight (see A Pause for Buddhism, p. 216).

Taoist practices like Qigong and Tai Chi use breath to move and cultivate Qi, or vital energy (see Embody, p. 119), while early Christian monks wove slow, conscious breathing into prayer for spiritual union. In indigenous and animistic cultures, breath is used in rituals, sweat lodges and shamanic journeys, to connect with ancestors and access healing.

> Breathwork has been used by psychologists and somatic therapists since the twentieth century to regulate the nervous system and release trauma. It has become especially popular in the last decade thanks to the work of Dutch extreme athlete Wim Hof, whose method combines cold exposure with controlled breathing and mental focus to reduce inflammation, boost metabolism and enhance physical and mental resilience. (For more on cold water immersion, see A Pause For Wild Swimming, p. 56).

Take an hour to breathe consciously

There are oodles of conscious breathing techniques available to try. For this hour, pick one of the three simple practices below that you can easily do alone in your chosen space. Each works in a slightly different way, but all use the breath to help your body relax and your mind settle, without stress on the system.

Three simple breathing techniques to try

ALTERNATE NOSTRIL BREATHING
Known in Sanskrit as Nadi Shodhana (meaning 'channel cleansing'), this balancing breath is a key exercise in Pranayama (yogic breathwork). As well as being relaxing, it is believed to balance the left and right sides of the brain, making it ideal for focus and emotional clarity.

Using your right thumb and ring finger:

- Close your right nostril and inhale through the left for a slow count of four.

- Hold the breath for a count of four.

- Close the left nostril and exhale through the right for a count of four.

- Then inhale through the right for four, keeping the breath low and steady.

- Hold gently for four.

- Close the right nostril and exhale through the left for four.

That completes one full round. Continue at a gentle, steady pace.

4–7–8 BREATHING

Used by pilots, first responders and people generally seeking calm quickly, this breath pattern was developed by integrative medicine pioneer Dr Andrew Weil in the early 2000s. Based on Pranayama techniques, its secret is the extended exhale, which is twice as long as the inhale.

- Inhale through your nose for a count of four.

- Hold the breath gently for a count of seven.

- Exhale slowly and steadily through your mouth for a count of eight.

Repeat for several cycles, or until you feel a sense of ease return.

BUTTERFLY BREATHING

This gentle practice is essentially a mindfulness exercise, particularly effective with children and teenagers who want to feel calm too.

- Inhale through your nose, and as you do, imagine a butterfly in a colour and pattern of your choice at the base of your spine, gently opening its wings.

- Hold the breath briefly.

- Exhale through your mouth, and as you breathe out, imagine the butterfly softly closing its wings.

- Let the exhale be just a little longer than the inhale, giving the butterfly time to settle. Repeat for ten breaths, or as long as you like or need.

When you have picked your practice, follow the steps below:

Breathing practice: Sit somewhere comfortable with your back supported, and allow your body to settle. Begin your chosen breath technique. Stay with the rhythm for as long as you feel comfortable, breathing gently and steadily. Stop at any point you need and return to start again with a clean new round.

Keeping time: Have an analogue clock close by, or your phone on airplane mode with the clock showing. To check the time at any point, feel free to open your eyes and glance at your clock, then close them gently again.

Rest and observe: When you have had enough, let go of the technique. Let your breath return to its natural pace. Notice any shifts in your body, breath or mood. Get up and have a glass of water if you need.

Breathing practice: Return to the same breath technique, stopping again when you need. Stay relaxed and steady. You might find the time goes quickly, or slowly. Just acknowledge any discomfort you might feel. Have patience.

Final rest: Let go of the technique, lie down or remain seated, and just be. Allow the calming effects of the practice to emanate. Nothing to do, nowhere to go. Just breathe naturally, before returning to your day.

Tips for a successful practice

- Choose a time and place where you won't be disturbed, so your body can fully settle into the rhythm of the breath, and make sure all your devices and notifications are off.

- Whichever practice you choose, try to use deep diaphragmatic breathing rather than shallow chest breathing. A good way to imagine this is to let your lower ribs and belly expand slightly as you inhale and soften as you exhale, like an accordion gently opening and closing.

- When you have practised for a while, try breathing with an open mouth for both the inhale and the exhale, which mimics more intense conscious breathwork and will feel more powerful. If you feel lightheaded or uncomfortable, return to nose breathing.

- Keep your breath gentle and unforced – comfort is more important than precision. If your nose is blocked up, use your mouth to breathe as and when you need.

Reflect on your practice

Later in the day or the next morning, check in with yourself. Do you feel any different? Try the technique once more for a few rounds – in bed, before you sleep, is a good place. Notice how your body responds.

Continue your practice

Try each of the different practices over the following weeks, and return to the one that feels best for a regular breathwork session. You might start with just a few rounds each morning and build up to taking longer. You could do this as soon as you wake to set you up for the day, before or after any regular morning practice you may have, or anytime during your schedule that works for you, your body and mood.

Therapeutic Breathwork: To go deeper, explore more, and move your breathing beyond regulation and into release, consider learning therapeutic breathwork. This helps us to release the emotional, physical and mental tension and trauma that we hold within our bodies, and to access the full potential of our breathing system. You can experience this in a one-to-one session, in a group workshop or on a retreat.

The main technique used by practitioners is Conscious Connected Breathwork. A rhythmic, continuous breathing practice with no pause between inhale and exhale, this has you breathe in and out through an open mouth to access 100 per cent of your respiratory system. It's safe and beneficial for most people, but if you have a health condition, ask your doctor before starting a regular practice.

Conscious Connected Breathwork can feel odd and uncomfortable at first, but because the combination completely occupies you on both a physical and mental level, you can't switch off (as you might do in a massage), or rationalise your feelings (as you might do in a counselling session). So you move through each emotion that comes up, releasing it, rather than getting stuck inside it and holding on to what you no longer need. It's one of the most powerful therapies I've ever experienced. For help finding a breathwork teacher, see Resources, p. 261.

Breathwork on hosted retreats

For total immersion, therapeutic breathwork retreats offer safe spaces in beautiful environments where you can learn Conscious Connected Breathwork and release stress and trauma in private, or group sessions, as part of a supportive community. To start off with something more low key, Yoga retreats where the teacher includes Pranayama (yogic breathwork) in the classes are an ideal place to learn, and witness first-hand, how using your breath can relax and support your mind and body. Research the Yoga teacher ahead of time if you don't know them, to ensure they include Pranayama in their sessions, as some do not.

RETREAT FOR A DAY
BE MINDFUL

'The present moment is all you ever have.' I still remember being struck by this sentence when I first read it in Eckhart Tolle's iconic book, *The Power of Now*. On a Thai beach in my twenties, footloose and excited on my first retreat in Asia, I had a pencil in my hand, underlining the best bits in my paperback version of it. Yes, yes, yes! I thought, the sunshine hot on my face, a fresh and glistening sea waiting beside me. The present moment *is* all I have – I may as well make the most of it. Which was easy, of course, on the island shores of Koh Samui. But not so easy on my return home to real life in a drizzly England.

It's not always straightforward to be in the present, as Billy Collins explores in his witty poem 'The Present', in which he writes:

> *It doesn't seem desirable or even possible*
> *to wake up every morning and begin*
> *leaping from one second into the next*
> *until you fall exhausted back into bed.*

This is why concentrated periods of being in the moment work best, which is what practising mindfulness is all about. To be fully present, rather than stuck in the past or fretting about the future. To give your full attention to what you are experiencing on a moment-to-moment basis. To be aware and awake to what you are doing, thinking and feeling, with acceptance, and without judgement or drama.

Though mindfulness has its roots in Buddhist Meditation (see A Pause for Buddhism, p. 216), you don't have to meditate to practise mindfulness. Mindfulness can simply be a useful way of being, developed by yourself, to draw on when you are agitated, distracted, confused or overwhelmed.

Mindfulness helps us:

- Notice and appreciate what's happening around us every day.
- Find it easier to focus and make fewer mistakes.
- Feel less stressed and react more calmly to things.
- Feel more peaceful and present.
- Handle discomfort or pain with more ease.

Take a day to try mindfulness, your way

Taking dedicated time out to devote yourself to being mindful can help you bring the practice more effectively into daily life. It's also a wonderful way to slow down and relax in the middle of a busy time.

Pepper your day with at least four clear mindfulness tasks, making at least one of them outside in nature. For ideas, see mindfulness tasks to try below. Then, for each task, practise how to be mindful.

How to be mindful: Start your activity, and while you are doing it, bring each of your five senses to bear on it in turn. What can you see, hear, smell, taste and touch while you are doing the task? Go through each of the senses, one by one, and answer yourself in your mind. Allow each question to have multiple answers.

Your thoughts will naturally wander. When you notice that they do, bring your attention back to your task by focusing again on one of your senses. When you have finished, stop your activity and close your eyes. How do you feel? Be present to the moment that you have put yourself in.

When I choose to be mindful while making a cup of tea and drinking it, for example, I might at first consciously see the decorated teapot I am filling with hot water. I might notice its colour, shape and pattern, perhaps a slight tannin stain on its rim. I might smell the fresh green tea leaves I have chosen to make my tea from.

I might then feel the texture of the pink pottery cup as I get it down from the shelf, and the slight breeze on my cheek and the top of my arm from the open window beside me. I'll listen to a blackbird sing outside before I hear the high-pitched sound of my kettle as it comes to boil. Before I pour the water onto my tea leaves, I'll feel the heat and moisture of the steam in the air and near my nostrils, and smell the invigorating fragrance of the newly soaked green leaves.

While I wait for it to brew, I'll notice the grain of the mango-wood tray I'll use to carry my cup of tea into the garden. Then I'll notice my thoughts go elsewhere – to the email I've just written, or to the birthday card I need to remember to post this weekend, until my tea is brewed, when I bring myself back to the sensation of lifting the pot and pouring the liquid into my cup.

I carry on, checking into each of my senses as I add a treat to my tray with my tea, walk out to my garden, sit down, pour it out and savour the clean feel of the green tea in my throat before I get up to get on with my day.

Mindfulness tasks to try

Morning or evening routines: Slowly and mindfully brushing your teeth, having a bath or shower, getting dressed or ready for bed.

Self-care rituals: Slowly and mindfully doing just one thing that will help you relax, be it rubbing oil on your body or cream on your face, massaging your feet or your head, or a few simple stretches.

Daily domestic tasks: Washing up, tidying, cleaning a room, ironing or sorting laundry.

Preparing and savouring food and drink: From making a hot drink to creating a lavish meal, then paying full attention to the taste, texture and aroma while you enjoy them, slowly and without distractions.

Unusual chores: Practical tasks you might do only once in a while, such as polishing silver or gold objects; protecting wooden furniture or art with natural oils; handwashing a delicate item; refolding your linens; re-organising a cupboard.

Creative activities: From doodling, sketching and painting to collaging, crafting or knitting (see Be an artist, p. 108). Or you could simply open an art book, or go to an art gallery, and really look at one painting, then describe on paper or in your mind's eye what you see.

Solo games: Such as doing a jigsaw, having a go at a puzzle, or playing solitaire.

Movement: Things like Qigong, slow Yoga or steady swimming or walking can be mindfulness in motion (see Embody, p. 119).

Gardening: Get your hands in the soil, do some weeding, or plant up some pots or beds with seeds or bulbs (see Garden, p. 74).

Seasonal activities outside: Listen to birdsong, gather leaves or blossoms to press, collect sea glass or shells from a beach, pick wild berries for jam or nettles for tea.

Mindful listening or conversation: If you want company on your retreat day, you could practise deep listening with a friend or family member, or just listen with full attention to a piece of music, birdsong or other sounds in nature solo.

Suggested schedule

On waking: Scan your body. Close your eyes and, starting at your toes, slowly move your attention up through your body to your head. Notice the sensations in each area without judgement, using your breath as an anchor.

Morning: Do your first chosen mindfulness activity – this could be a regular practice you have, but done more slowly and with your full attention, or something new you have chosen. Make this something soft and easy, perhaps something you don't have to get out of your pyjamas for.

Late morning: Choose your second mindfulness activity, something longer and with more weight, ideally done outside.

Afternoon: Choose your third mindfulness activity. If you haven't been outside as yet, now is the time, or settle into a more creative activity. Then switch off entirely, doing something you love or that lifts you out of yourself, whether that's going for a vigorous bike ride or watching some comedy.

Evening: After an evening meal, choose your fourth mindfulness activity, something that will help you relax and wind down before sleep.

A PAUSE FOR JAPANESE RITUALS

There are several gorgeous Japanese rituals that fully embody mindfulness, and are easy to weave into daily life. Try inventing your own version of the suggestions below:

- ***Shinrin-yoku* (forest bathing):** Developed in 1980s Japan to counteract urban stress, this therapeutic practice of mindfully immersing yourself in a forest or woodland draws on centuries of Shinto and Buddhist respect for forests as sacred spaces.

Try it: Take a slow walk in your nearby forest, park, or wooded area, engaging your senses to notice sounds, smells and textures, and breathing deeply to foster calm. Inhale the phytoncides released by trees to boost your immune system.

- *Shodō* **(calligraphy):** Dating back to the sixth century, this mindful practice of writing characters with brush and ink evolved from Chinese calligraphy into a Zen-influenced art, where practitioners focus on each deliberate stroke, and the flow of their breath and movement.
Try it: Slowly write a soothing word or phrase with a favourite pen, pencil or brush, paying attention to the shape of each letter and your breathing as your hand moves.

- *Ikebana* **(flower arranging):** Beginning in the seventh century as Buddhist floral offerings, *Ikebana* developed into a refined art embodying harmony and simplicity, with the practitioner focusing on the balance and placement of each and every stem. **Try it:** Arrange flowers or branches slowly in a treasured jug or vase, focusing on shape and balance, and the movement of your breath.

- *Chadō* **(tea ceremony):** Traditionally held in serene tea houses or tranquil garden settings across Japan, this is a graceful ritual where every step of

> making and drinking tea is performed with mindful intention. The ceremonies take place year-round, with each season bringing its own touches to the utensils, flowers, and sweets served. **Try it:** Prepare tea slowly and deliberately, focusing on each sense as you do. Serve in a favourite cup, and savour the taste.

Tips for a successful practice

- ✧ This is a day to settle in, but don't take it or yourself too seriously during your mindful tasks or between times.

- ✧ If you struggle to focus on things in general, start with a very easy, everyday task and spend only a few minutes focusing on your senses. Build up to spending more time, ideally doing something you truly love to do.

- ✧ At any point you like during your day, for added poise, try mindfulness pioneer Dr Jon Kabat-Zinn's rather wonderful Dignity suggestion from his book *Wherever You Go, There You Are*: 'Try sitting with dignity for thirty seconds. Note how you feel. Try standing with dignity. Where are your shoulders? How is your spine, your head? What would it mean to walk with dignity?'

Reflect on your practice

Mindfulness helps you, quite literally, come to your senses. The relaxed, calmer state that follows being fully present can help you tap into your sixth sense, or intuition, and with that can come solutions to things with which you might have been struggling. Allow yourself to harvest this clarity. Have your journal or loose paper to hand during and after your day to jot down any ideas, and take time during the week that follows to do the same.

Continue your practice

You can choose to bring your five senses to bear on any task in your day, whenever you want, to bring you back to the present moment and give yourself the chance of calm and clarity. If you are particularly overwhelmed, even a few minutes of being mindful, somewhere quiet, and focusing on what you can see, hear, smell, touch and taste, can ground you enough to carry on with your day.

Going forward, there can be a real pleasure in being mindful during simple, everyday tasks. My massage therapist Sophia, for example, says she likes to 'get my washing in, or put it out to dry, because the fresh smell of washing is homely and comforting, and instantly takes me back to my mum'.

Practising situational mindfulness can also be useful to help us cope with difficult experiences in life. We can approach a stressful event or an uncomfortable conversation, for example, with our full presence, and without judgement, rather than being on auto pilot or reacting with unnecessary emotion in a way we might usually do.

Note that mindfulness doesn't have to be done solo. Being fully present with a friend or family member can be hugely enriching, whether you are making art, dancing or enjoying a drink in the sunshine.

Hosted mindfulness retreats

Mindfulness retreats come in many forms, from mindful movement and walking retreats to silent forest immersions and conscious eating retreats. Some include embodied movement practices that bring attention to your breath and moment-by-moment experience, such as Yoga and Qigong (see Embody, p. 119), and many are set beside natural water to contemplate beside or swim in. Choose secular mindfulness retreats that focus on cultivating presence in daily activities, or Buddhist retreats if you want to learn and practise more formal mindful Meditation (see A Pause For Buddhism, p. 216). Dr Kabat-Zinn runs mindfulness retreats online (for more on mindfulness, see Resources, p. 261).

RETREAT FOR LONGER
GO INTO SILENCE

Have you ever noticed how silence can be a companion to clarity and calm? Being in silence is my go-to, and I give myself regular doses of it. This doesn't mean I don't appreciate life's beautiful cacophony – I just prefer to choose when to experience it, so I can fully engage. Having grown up in a large noisy family, I once felt fearful of silence. Perhaps it's something you also feel uneasy about? If so, it might be a good time to experience just how replenishing it can be.

Silence has been practised in monastic traditions for thousands of years, as a way to slow down and reconnect with a higher purpose. But it doesn't have to be seen as a religious or spiritual pursuit, or as giving something up. It's a route that can help us face our true nature with honesty, be in the world with more attention and clarity, and live a more enjoyable life. Once we get the hang of it, it can be a delicious experience in and of itself. As Norwegian explorer Erling Kagge says in his book *Silence: In the Age of Noise*: 'Silence in itself is rich. It is exclusive and luxurious.'

We need courage to go into silence. At first, the internal 'noise' we find in a quieter environment can be deafening. Our thoughts and feelings cancel out anything we can actually see or hear. We can feel scared and lonely. We realise how much we distract ourselves in our daily lives, by scrolling on social media, binge watching films, turning to alcohol, sugar, sex or other people, gossiping or just talking incessantly.

Such distractions offer us temporary relief from our realities but they also stop us getting to know ourselves and making any meaningful change. As time passes in silence, we start to settle inside. We find the space to intuit where we are at in our lives, and what we may need, away from everyday chatter. This introspection can be challenging, sometimes revealing difficult truths, which is why many people struggle with the solitude that silence brings.

Being in silence can give us:

- Deep calm, mental clarity and relief from inner chaos.
- Honest self-reflection and gentle self-compassion.
- Emotional and physical replenishment.
- Stronger connection with nature, stillness and gratitude in daily life.
- Clearer intuition, fresh perspectives and enhanced creativity.

Experience a weekend in silence

Start by setting an intention to enter into a weekend of silence willingly. It's important that we choose our silence, as the ancient desert hermits would have done. This way we feel in control of it, and able to use it to our advantage, rather than disappearing into a lonely space. What results is a very different experience to the fearful, lonely places that might be faced by lost mountaineers, say, or exiles and prisoners.

Next, understand how to be silent during your weekend, which will in turn help you decide what you will do with your time. This isn't about just having a quiet weekend, but giving yourself a chance to truly listen and go inward. To relish and engage with your chosen peace, rather than distract yourself from it. Read 'Ways to be silent' below, then devise yourself a schedule.

Ways to be silent

Stop talking: Silence is defined as a 'complete absence of sound', and the easiest way to enter it for a short period of time is to simply stop talking to other people. Many people find the idea of this scary and uncomfortable. But while we are social creatures who need interaction with others, gifting ourselves a break from them can enrich those interactions. Silence gifts us the clarity and presence to engage in a more meaningful, intentional way, and reconnects us with ourselves.

Limit engagement: Tell others you are taking time out. Switch off your phone and other electronic devices, and put them away. If you have a landline, unplug it. You can pick up messages after your weekend. Avoid conversation, but know it's okay to not be totally silent yourself. Whilst you won't be consciously speaking or seeking out company, if, when you are out, someone says hello to you, you'll naturally want to respond. It's a silence within rather than without that you are aiming to create – a sustainable stillness of thought and focus which, if found, is not going to be disturbed by saying hello or thanking someone briefly.

Limit external noise: Putting yourself in quiet surroundings helps you engage with silence. In our contemporary world we can't usually control other people's noise, but we can control our own. Just for one weekend, choose to switch off anything in your chosen retreat space that creates noise, including the radio and TV as well as your digital devices. If you want to garden, don't cut the hedge with a strimmer or mow your lawn, for instance. Don't drive unless it's truly necessary. If you need to play music, choose pieces and tracks that complement your silence, rather than distract you from it. Get yourself some earplugs if you have noisy neighbours.

Limit internal noise: 'Sound' extends beyond the physical noise of a fridge buzzing, a car horn tooting or loud music playing, to our daily engagement with all stimuli. Even seemingly quiet activities, such as recording, writing, reading, watching films, scrolling, checking messages and taking notes or photographs can be far from silent, because of the busyness that our words and thoughts create. Such activities can agitate and distract you, taking you away from listening to what's going on inside your internal space.

As your devices will be off, you won't be scrolling, messaging or watching anything. But also avoid all types of other writing except for journalling. If you can't bear the thought of not reading, avoid materials that agitate you, and avoid escaping into a book for hours. Be with your silence rather than trying to ignore it.

Noble Silence: When we refrain from engagement and communication with intention in this way, we are drawing on the Buddhist practice of Noble Silence. This helps create a sustainable stillness and awareness within you that, with practice, remains undisturbed by outside distractions. The idea is also that some matters are best approached through direct experience of the self, rather than through debate with others (see A Pause for Buddhism, p. 216).

Journalling: This is one form of writing that we can allow ourselves inside our silence on this retreat, as a gentle way to offload and reflect on how we are feeling and what we are thinking throughout. Rather than reaching for your phone to talk to someone, reach for your journal – or a loose piece of paper – and write down what you want to ask or say – to yourself, someone else, or just the universe. In Noble Silence on a hosted Buddhist retreat, you would avoid even journalling, so, in this spirit, plan to avoid it on day two if you can.

Being mindful: Tune in, slow down and be present. When we are in silence, we become more attuned to our surroundings, experiencing the world through all five senses. We notice the fragrance of our morning coffee, the cobalt blue of a patch of sky bordered by elephant-grey clouds, and other subtle details of daily life.

For absorbing entertainment, scatter your day with mindful activities that resonate with you to enjoy this process (see Be mindful, p. 199, for ideas). Avoid starting new projects or making grand gestures – keep things easy and light.

Going out in silence: Just because you are in silence does not mean you have to stay in. Going out but remaining quiet can be a powerful, motivating experience. It can be enlightening to just listen, sense and watch while everyone else is being busy and making noise. Finding silence in the bigger world is a way to know that, in the future, whenever you choose, you can go there and be silent again too.

To give yourself the best chance of enjoying and staying in your silence while you are out, be intentional about the activity you choose, and design it before you leave your house – where you will go and roughly how long you might take. It's best to avoid eating out during your silent weekend.

Going for a walk (see A Pause For Walking, p. 30) or forest bathing (see A Pause For Japanese Rituals, p. 203) are easy choices. But if you're in an urban area, quiet can be found in unexpected places too. Find a bench in a courtyard, a pew in a church, or a room in a museum or gallery that appeals to you. Choose silence when you enter, even if others are talking. If a space feels too busy, simply move on to another.

Suggested Schedule

Day one: Move into silence

On waking: Allow yourself to wake naturally with no alarm, then take the time to listen. What can you hear? Be aware of any external noises as well as your own thoughts. Start to savour the silence. Next, scan your body. Close your eyes and, starting at your toes, slowly move your attention up through your body to your head, noticing the sensations in each area without judgement, using your breath as an anchor.

Morning: Take things slowly. Do a chosen mindful activity in your chosen retreat space to get used to being in quiet. Afterwards, sit with yourself in silence somewhere comfortable for 30 minutes or so. Challenge yourself to do nothing, simply to be. You can close your eyes or keep them open. Afterwards, let the feeling resonate. Write about whatever has come up in your journal or on loose paper if you want to.

Afternoon: After lunch, head out into the world, staying inside your silence. At some point while you are out, find a place to ground yourself in nature. Be barefoot on grass for a few minutes, or sense the grounding presence of a mature tree beside you. Close your eyes and imagine you also have roots, extending from your feet deep down into the earth. Imagine you are releasing all your tension into the soil, knowing that the earth can take it.

Evening: Reflect on your day, either in your journal or your mind, starting with the sentence. 'Being in silence feels . . .' Ask yourself what you have missed, what you have enjoyed, what you might do differently tomorrow. Return to your morning mindful activity, or choose a different one. If you feel restless, go for a short walk. Indulge in an early night.

Day two: Deepen the experience

On waking: Allow yourself to wake naturally again. Stay lying down a little longer today before rising, to simply listen and observe. Practise the body scan from 'On waking' in Day one, then do any regular morning practice you may have. In the spirit of Noble Silence (see p. 211), resist journalling this morning. Try instead for a day for wordlessness and presence.

Morning: Settle into stillness with a longer period of seated silence this time, in a space that feels warm and comfortable, from 60 to 90 minutes. Sit with no goal other than to be, without any task. Let thoughts come and go without chasing them or trying to stop them. This may feel challenging or easeful. Welcome either feeling. When you have had enough, stretch your body out.

Afternoon: Have your main meal at lunchtime, then take a walk in silence, somewhere familiar but with no destination. This is not a walk to get somewhere but a quiet wandering. Let your senses guide you – notice trees shaking in the wind, feel the warmth of the sun or the chill of the air, be alert to everything you can hear and smell, look up and relish any small details in your surroundings. Pause when you feel like it. Let the world come to you, but retain your own quiet.

Evening: Resist the urge to fill the quiet and do things. Just rest, then make your evening meal, something you enjoy that doesn't require much effort. If you want to, journal honestly, but not for long, perhaps starting with, 'Today I noticed . . .' Or draw something that expresses how you feel, rather than using words. Sleep when your body is ready.

The day after your weekend: Ease very gently back into talking and the buzz of the world. Keep noise and chat to a minimum for as long as you can. This isn't the time to call up someone you haven't spoken to in a while, deal with a difficult situation at work, or embark on a stressful journey. Save those things for tomorrow, or later. If you have more time, simply carry on being in silence.

Tips for a successful practice

- Avoid distractions. This includes everything you might usually distract yourself with, such as sugar and alcohol as well as TV and electronic devices. For advice on unplugging, see Unplug p. 177.

- Allow discomfort. You may well feel restless and agitated at times, even anxious or frightened, and as the day goes on, a certain 'stickiness' and resistance may set in. Stay with it. See what this discomfort is trying to tell you.

- ✧ Know it's okay if your surroundings are not wholly quiet. If you were on a retreat in India, for example, you might notice the grounds are tranquil, yet hear in the distance dogs barking, cockerels crowing, men drumming and women singing as they thud their washing on bare rocks. Listen to other people's noise, even enjoy it, but then carry on inside your silence.

Reflect on your practice

After your time in silence, notice how things are. Has the heightened awareness of simple things you cultivated over the weekend helped you return to daily interactions with greater presence and depth? Are you relishing the noise of humanity, with more joy and appreciation? Or do you just feel agitated and annoyed?

During your silence, you may have started to sense that the way out of any issues is through them. Ask yourself, what is it that you need in your life now? What am I missing? What am I hungry for? Sometimes useful revelations that we are not expecting emerge after time in silence.

Continue your practice

You can feel the luxury of silence whenever you need in your daily life. Find a tranquil spot, switch off your digital media and just listen. If you cannot find external quiet, find it internally. Stop talking, slow down, be. Afterwards, be aware of your thoughts and feelings, writing them down if it's helpful.

Regularly, get away from words. Decide not to answer the phone, start a solo hobby, or seek out somewhere tranquil each day, such as a stretch of water or a beautiful view. If you feel you've got little time, just stop for a minute or two, and listen to the silence of your home when alone, without being afraid of it.

To pursue silence further, schedule in regular silent days at home, a special 24 hours away at a guesthouse, or go on an immersive silent retreat.

Hosted silent retreats

It is magical to be in silence together with others, supported in an organised setting and nourished by the energy of a group. Some Yoga, Meditation, life coaching and general wellbeing retreats schedule pockets of silence into the daily programme, to help their guests calm down, process what they are going through, and experience the clarity that silence can bring. Guests are often encouraged to stay in silence until after breakfast, for example, or to have quiet afternoons where people are encouraged to relax together but not to 'chat' – and certainly not to scroll.

For fully silent, structured retreats held in Noble Silence (see p. 211), try a Buddhist retreat (see A Pause For Buddhism below). They have sharing circles, helpful teachers and inspiring evening talks to support you. Why not start with a day retreat and build up to a longer stay? Such silent retreats can be a challenging and restless experience at first, but I have always left them with an unexpected feeling of contentedness and lightness. This inspired my poem 'Silent Retreat at Gaia House', which I wrote following many a stay at the retreat in Devon, England (see p. 276).

A PAUSE FOR BUDDHISM

All three retreats in this Settle chapter are in part inspired by Buddhism, a practical philosophy for living well that is increasingly appealing to people of any faith, including atheists and agnostics. With its emphasis on letting go, being mindful, cultivating compassion, finding quiet and attempting to live in the present, rather than staying stuck in the past or fretting about the future, it feels like a true antidote to our contemporary overwhelm.

Buddhism began over 2,500 years ago in northern India, when, according to legend, a young prince named Siddhartha Gautama, troubled by the reality of old age, sickness and death, slipped away from his palace in the dead of night (as you do). In Buddhist thought, these universal experiences are all part of *samsara* – the endless cycle of suffering and rebirth that everyone is caught up in. Leaving behind his wealth, wife and newborn son, Gautama set out as an ascetic, determined to understand the roots of such suffering and how to overcome them.

After years of searching, he apparently realised that suffering isn't caused by life's ups and downs themselves but by our attachment to them – our clinging, craving and resistance to change. By seeing things clearly and letting go, he found a path to lasting peace and became the 'Buddha', which in both Sanskrit and Pali means 'awakened one'. His teachings have rippled across the world ever since, taking root in nations all across Asia, and, in recent decades, much of the West.

At its heart, Buddhism isn't about gods or dogma, but an intentional way of living, known as following the *dharma*, which is laid out in what is called the Eightfold Path: right view (seeing things clearly, not making assumptions), right intention (acting kindly, not selfishly), right speech (being honest, not gossiping), right action (not harming others by stealing or cheating), right livelihood (work that doesn't harm people or the planet), right effort (building good habits), right mindfulness (being aware of your thoughts and feelings) and right concentration (focusing fully on what you're doing). Linking everything is the concept of non-attachment (see A Pause For Letting Go, p. 130).

Buddhist Meditation methods, such as Vipassana, Tibetan and Zen, help develop this intentional way of living by focusing on concentration (on the breath, an image or a question) and enquiry (into who we are and what life's really like). Loving Kindness Meditation helps cultivate compassion (see Be kind, p. 82). Many hosted Buddhist retreats across the globe are open to beginners and non-Buddhists, so that you can learn to meditate and immerse yourself in the Buddhist way in a supportive community, and, often, in Noble Silence. For more information about Buddhist philosophy, please see Resources, p. 261.

PLAN

'Let's build a life we can live in'
Cleo Wade, *that sounds great*

Would you like a day that includes moments that matter, as well as realistic priorities? To streamline easier choices, so you have space for the more interesting ones? Or perhaps you would like to plan a whole new life for yourself and open up new possibilities.

To plan means to think about and arrange the details of something before it happens. In the context of retreating, this is more than just filling a calendar or making a to do list. It's about intentionally shaping your time and energy, to create a life that feels meaningful and manageable. Planning then becomes a restorative practice for self-care and growth.

Today, people value how well we bring together teams, technology and systems to get things done efficiently and come up with new ideas. On a retreat, we can soften this perspective, and view planning as an act of personal courage and clarity.

Taking time out to organise ourselves allows us to step out of overwhelm and into intention. It helps us create a roadmap to guide us towards the life we want to live.

How much time do you have to retreat?

- An hour – Design your day (p. 221)
- A day – Trim your choices (p. 226)
- Longer – Re-imagine your life (p. 235)

Whatever you choose, refer to the Retreat Toolkit (p. 15) to help you prepare for each retreat.

Start with a check-in

Write in your journal or think to yourself:

- *I like/don't like to plan ahead because . . .*
- *Choices I make daily that feel stressful/joyful include . . .*
- *I'd like to change something about my lifestyle/relationship/ friendships/career/something else . . .*

RETREAT FOR AN HOUR
DESIGN YOUR DAY

How do you usually design your day? Some people like to go with the flow. Others to treat their day like a military operation. You may be keen on making lists, but, like me, put far too much on them, imagining you will be able to climb a mountain when all you might manage is a grassy hillock.

How we set up our day can have a big impact on how we feel during it, and what we get done. It matters because how we spend our mornings, afternoons and evenings is, after all, how we spend our lives.

There are oodles of ways to plan that have been devised by coaches and psychologists. To keep things simple, I'd like to share the most useful steps I've picked up from career and life coaching retreats of various kinds. These are easy, timeless, and don't require any special setup.

Simple steps to help design your day

Focus on just three things each day: Pick just three things you need to do, so you keep things calm and achievable. Cognitive psychology research shows our brains can only manage a few meaningful tasks at once, and that three is a sweet spot that supports clarity, focus and follow-through.

Start with what matters first: Plan by priority, not by time, and start with what's most important to you. This way, even if the day gets messy, something vital is already done. We often underestimate how long things will take – a common thinking trap known as the 'planning fallacy'.

Do less, but do it well: Let go of the idea that you have to do everything. Plan to focus your energy where it matters most. Doing fewer things, with more attention, leads to better results and more satisfaction.

Do one thing at a time: It's tempting to juggle. But multitasking is a brain drain that scatters your focus, slows you down and increases your risk of making mistakes. Our brains work best when we give one task our full attention.

Write down loose ends: Unfinished tasks tug at your attention all day and create mental tension, until we capture or close them – a pattern called the 'Zeigarnik Effect'. Jot them down somewhere in a separate, ongoing list, so you can come back to them when the time is right.

Adjust your plan if you need to: Check your plan during the day, and if something isn't working, move things around. The habit of reviewing and adapting as you go is known as 'reflective practice', and it helps you stay realistic, flexible and make better decisions.

Schedule in wellbeing breaks: These are your daily non-negotiables. What you need to do, for your health and wellbeing, to have a sane, enjoyable and productive day. Ideally they will include movement and rest, away from a screen and the hustle and bustle of life. Decide what they are, put them in your calendar, and see them as meetings that you can't cancel.

My daily non-negotiables are my Meditation and Yoga, either a walk or a swim, an evening family meal, and any health and wellbeing appointments I might have booked. For you, it might be to go for a run, have an evening surf, browse in a bookshop, attend a gig, have a massage, bathe your children or have a coffee with someone special.

Take an hour to map out your day

Take an hour to practise designing your day. If you choose to do this more regularly, it will become a quicker process over time. You could do this first thing in the morning, for the day ahead, or in an afternoon or evening, for your tomorrow.

Settle: Start by settling yourself somewhere comfortable, where you're unlikely to be disturbed, and get out your journal or loose paper.

Select: Next, mindfully select the three most important tasks for your day. If it's easier, write down lots of ideas at first, then pare these back to the most important three. Write them down, with numbers beside them, one below the other, putting the most important item first.

List: Jot down any loose ends on a separate list – thoughts or to-dos that are on your mind but aren't priorities right now.

Arrange: Draw three columns and label them To Do → In Progress → Done. Place your three key tasks, perhaps on sticky notes, in the first column. As you move through the day, you'll move each one across to the next column. There's something deeply satisfying about watching your intentions move towards completion.

Diarise: Choose what you will do for your wellbeing breaks. Add them to your calendar as appointments you have booked with yourself. If you need the motivation, you could treat them as 'to do' tasks and add them to your first column as well.

Check: Then check over your plan to make sure you've got your priorities right. Remind yourself you can revise the plan as your day unfolds, before getting on with your morning. Follow your design throughout your day.

Tips for a successful practice

- Know that using pen and paper is the best way to do this exercise mindfully, without distractions.

- Stay flexible. As the day goes on, move your tasks across your columns. Adapt to what's happening, and adjust your task list as you need. Notice if you're struggling to do a task, and ask yourself if it really needs to be done, today or ever. Letting go of things is part of designing your day, too (see Say no, p. 169).

- Lists have a role when they are finite, such as shopping lists – so use them as you see fit. Keep your 'loose end' list near to hand, so you can add to it as things occur to you, and so you don't get distracted from your three chosen tasks, or from replenishing yourself on your wellbeing breaks.

Reflect on your practice

At the end of your day, ask yourself, how has your day been? Has planning it this morning helped you have an easier day, or do you feel more pressured? If the latter, your tasks may have been too large to tackle realistically. For help simplifying choices, see Trim your choices, p. 226, or if you sense there is something more fundamental you need to change, see Re-imagine your life, p. 235.

Continue your practice

If you like this way of designing your day, carry on immediately. Take anything that you did not get done today and use it to help you start tomorrow's plan. You can carry on using the method to plan each day – or to plan what your three most important goals are for the week, or the month, or the season ahead.

There are online apps that allow you to manage your day too, but I find using paper keeps the process more mindful, and makes for a quieter, gentler way to begin my day away from a screen. That said, if it helps, you could keep your 'loose ends' list in the notes section of your phone or online, so it's easy to update, delete, change and add to throughout your week.

RETREAT FOR A DAY
TRIM YOUR CHOICES

I have a picture of a pebble-floored, wooden-beamed room in Rhodes torn from a magazine in My Simplicity Book (see p. 158). There's an oak desk, graced by a bunch of wild cyclamen, and, through the window behind it, an astonishing ocean view. It's the hideaway of a designer – let's call her Eve – who, according to the feature, wears the same type of shirt every day. Next to the photo of her serene home office there's a row of these white linen shirts neatly hung behind her. She stocks up on her favourite style, she says, to avoid wasting time choosing what to wear. So she can get on with being creative – or, presumably, gazing at that sea.

Eve's story reminds me of travelling, where you have only a suitcase, rucksack or holdall to put all your things. When you move through life with less, you have fewer choices, and this brings a sense of ease (see Declutter your stuff, p. 58). Do you feel overwhelmed by choices you have to make every day? For many of us, daily decisions – like what to wear or eat – can be overwhelming, especially when there are endless options. Limiting them not only reduces mental clutter and makes planning easier, but helps liberate us for the more interesting things in life. As Henry David Thoreau says in *Walden*, his transcendentalist memoir of simple living: 'Our life is frittered away by detail. Simplify, simplify.'

Simplifying our choices is important because our brains have a limited capacity to process information. Overusing them reduces our ability to think clearly and make the right decisions. Trimming trivial choices gives us more energy for exciting ones, like picking a gig to attend or planning an adventurous trip, and for decisions that truly matter, from career moves to relationships. It also gives us greater satisfaction. Ever felt overwhelmed by a huge restaurant menu? Often, life is more enjoyable with fewer options.

Too many decisions also agitate us emotionally, because decision-making and self-control use the same resource, making us irritable and impulsive when we're exhausted. Struggling with choice reveals a disconnection from ourselves, whereas learning to trust our instincts is empowering. Since the contemporary world won't limit choices for us anytime soon, we can take control.

Limiting choice:

- Reduces mental load so our brains cope better.
- Makes us nicer to be around.
- Lowers anxiety and increases our sense of satisfaction.
- Creates space for fun stuff and what truly matters.
- Builds self-trust.

Take a day to simplify your choices

This is a 'working' retreat day, but know that, afterwards, your life is likely to feel more easeful. Making decisions can be agitating, so pepper your day with delightful things to give yourself joy, and take yourself on an outing when you need to shift your energy. When you do, challenge yourself not to deliberate on trivial choices– take *this* path through the park, listen to *that* piece of music while you walk, have *this* dish for lunch. Make clean choices as practice for the weeks and months ahead.

Today you'll take the morning to write down the regular decisions you tend to make. This will help you to reflect on just how many there are, and which ones feel most stressful. In the afternoon, you'll work out ways to streamline the most overwhelming ones, or get rid of those that don't matter altogether.

Making and recording your decisions in this way helps prevent energy-draining overthinking. You could look at streamlining all your regular life decisions, or the those you need to make in a shorter timeframe of, say, the next day or week. There may be choices you simply want to banish from your life forever, or ask someone else to make, especially if they relate to a shared household. Your list and notes will be supremely personal to you and what you find challenging.

Ideas for regular life choices

Children or other dependants: Daily routines, activities, meals, other ways to support their needs.

Cleaning and tidying: Where to keep things, which household products to use, how often and who tidies, cleans and launders.

Clothing: Outfits to choose for work, relaxation, going out, exercise and so on. When and how often to buy essentials such as underwear and nightwear. When to take a shopping trip to find a winter coat, a summer swimming costume, or an outfit for a special event, such as an upcoming party or wedding, and what to buy.

Daily routines: Morning and evening tasks, routes to work and school, where to put your recycling and so on.

Digital habits: When to check messages, which app to open first, when to turn it all on and switch it all off, what to delete.

Food and drink: What to have for breakfast, lunches at home, packed lunches, evening meals and snacks, hot and cold drinks, where to eat and drink when you go out.

Fun and free time: How and when to recharge, indulge in hobbies, enjoy weekends, go out, or find quiet, relaxing time.

Gardening: Regular tasks that need doing, and who does them, from watering and weeding to planting and storing.

Greetings: Who and how to send messages to, for birthdays and other key events. How to acknowledge people in your local area you see daily, from the postman to a barista.

Life admin: When and how to file key documents, pay bills, make to do lists, set reminders and so on.

Media: What and what not to read, watch and listen to, and when.

Pet care: Feeding, walking, grooming, vet checks.

Wellbeing: The how, what and when for regular health checks, one-off treatments, morning practices, daily exercise, haircuts, skincare rituals and products, supplements and medications.

Suggested schedule

On waking: Start while your mind is fresh. Sit up in bed or somewhere else comfy, take your journal or loose paper and list the areas of your life for which you make daily, weekly and monthly decisions. Use the Ideas for regular life choices above to help you, making up your own headings and putting them in an order that suits you.

Morning: After breakfast, look at your list. Underneath each of your life areas, jot down the regular decisions you make related to them. Work quickly, without overthinking, then take a break.

On your return, look at your lists and ask yourself, which decisions feel easy and obvious, and which feel too numerous or overwhelming? Is there something you want to streamline, or decide not to do altogether? Circle the difficult decisions you immediately spot. Many people, for example, find many of their decisions related to clothing and food the most challenging. Then put down your pen and take a substantial break, ideally by moving outside in the fresh air.

Afternoon: After lunch, sit somewhere else delightful for a change of scene and return to your list. Continue to circle all the regular decisions you find difficult or overwhelming until you feel a sense of completion.

Then work through these circled decisions, one by one, and make the choices you can now, on paper, so that when these tasks come round again in your life, you have already thought them through and, if need be, trimmed them down. Wherever possible, make just one choice for each decision. When a decision feels too daunting to make now, just write 'pass' and move on.

You might start with quick wins, adding notes for anything you need to do to make them happen. For example, if one of your life areas is food, you might write: 'evening meal for our busy Tuesday nights – soup or veg curry (make/buy a stash for freezer). Other weekday evening meals – Pass', and so on.

After a break, circle the items you have written 'pass' beside, which are usually the most stressful. Choose just one of these to tackle today, using these tips below:

- ✧ Narrow it down. Try listing three choices you *could* make, then make a short pros and cons list for each of them to help you decide on just one.

- ✧ Change your space. Go and stand in the actual place you usually make these decisions to spark ideas, whether that's by your fridge, desk, wardrobe or somewhere else.

- ✧ Less is more. Simply doing less helps make choices easier. Are there things in your life can you simply cut out? (for help doing so, see Say no, p. 169).

If you are planning what you eat, for example, you could start with the most stressful meal of the day, which for me is evening meals. You could create a simple weekly menu on this retreat day, and plan to follow it for a month, after which you could refresh it to keep things interesting. For meal ideas, look through cookbooks you have, or reflect on favourite meals you've had out that you could recreate at home.

Evening: Review your lists and do what feels right to create a sense of completion for today. Tidy them up, write out clean copies of your decisions, pin them to your fridge or by your desk. If you feel inspired, work through other decisions you have 'passed' on, or commit to revisiting them later by making a date with yourself in your diary.

Before bed, bring to mind one clear decision you have made today that has made you feel more free. A shorter timeframe in which to check your morning messages? An obvious choice of lunch for an event this Saturday? Tap into that feeling of freedom before you turn out the light.

Tips for a successful practice

- ✧ Resist perfectionism and overthinking. You can always change your mind later. Let ease inform your choices. For example, if you're planning a morning routine – do you add an extra domestic task, or give yourself the chance of arriving at work earlier? Be kind to yourself and choose the more relaxing choice.

- ✧ If you are really stuck, ask someone you trust what they think after your retreat day, but reserve the right to ignore their advice.

- ✧ If you are overwhelmed by regular decisions, plan another retreat day to work through them. If you need help with your clothes, see A Pause for the Capsule Wardrobe, p. 63. For help with managing your digital devices, see Unplug, p. 177. If you are overwhelmed by disorder in your home, see Declutter your stuff, p. 58.

- ✧ Save big decisions for another time. For this one day, focus on streamlining regular choices and routines. If a choice feels too complex, note it down to revisit later – see tips below for dealing with bigger decisions.

Reflect on your practice

On waking the next morning, see if your unconscious has worked on your lists overnight, and jot down anything important. Is there anything obvious you'd like to add, especially to those daunting choices? Your mind will keep working on your lists and choices in the coming days, so keep paper to hand so you can jot down any fresh ideas. If it's working for you, continue to modify your lists until you feel happy with your everyday choices, and, ideally, until there are no more 'passes'.

Continue your practice

If you find this practice frees up time and energy, make it a regular activity. Refer to your list of choices whenever you need, especially in moments of overwhelm. Adjust your headings as your needs and lifestyle evolve, making fresh new lists that serve you. Being away on holiday, or on a hosted retreat of any kind, is an ideal time to trim your at-home choices, when you are removed from any daily stresses, can see things from a distance, and have more time for pondering and planning. Take a notebook with you if you're stuck with a particular decision and see what unfolds.

A PAUSE FOR HANDLING BIGGER DECISIONS

When you have trimmed your regular choices, you are free to use your new-found energy for more exciting ones, from organising a weekend getaway to choosing a comedy act to go to. You'll also be freer to make decisions that truly matter, such as choosing an educational course or changing jobs. Here are three suggestions for how to deal with bigger, and sometimes more difficult, decisions:

- **Use the 10/10/10 rule:** Ask yourself how you will feel about this decision in 10 minutes, 10 months and 10 years. Write down the answers in your journal. This helps you move beyond your emotional, impulsive responses and come up with something that serves you better.

- **Give your unconscious mind some space:** Psychologists agree that unconscious thought processes can lead to better decisions in complex situations. Sleep on it, go for a walk, step outside – do anything unrelated to the decision at hand. This will give you time to process before you make a firm commitment.

- **Ask every part of you:** If you're especially stuck, I love this idea created by Canada-based midlife vitality coach Tania Carrière. 'The feeling of being stuck is usually because one of your inner voices is too loud and not letting everyone else speak, or everyone is speaking at once,' she explains. This exercise allows you to create calm and intention by engaging each inner voice individually:

- First make a list of all the 'me's that you want involved in your decision. You might have a 'fun-loving me', a 'responsible me', a 'weary me', an 'optimistic me'. Sometimes there might be a few borrowed 'me's that sound like a parent, wise aunt, older sibling or the boss.

- Write each 'me' on a different piece of paper. Next, clearly articulate your question – the thing you want their opinion on – such as 'How should I be balancing my time differently?' or 'Should I leave my job?'

- Your challenge is to spend five minutes with each of your 'me's, giving yourself advice from only the perspective of the persona. If it helps, you could place your 'personas' on different chairs around your home and/or garden, and sit in the chair as that persona for each of your five minutes.

- Journal the answer or speak it out loud. By the end, you will have sat in all the chairs, opened your perspective and heard from the whole Advisory Board of you. Inevitably you will have found momentum too, as you will clearly 'hear' the advice that you had to give yourself all along.

RETREAT FOR LONGER
RE-IMAGINE YOUR LIFE

As the author of your story, how do you want the next chapter to go? Is there something about your life that isn't quite working for you, that you'd like to re-imagine? To re-imagine is to visualise possibilities, especially for what lies ahead. If we take time to do so, with care and intention, we will feel inspired to act on our new visions.

The practice of coaching is packed with enticing but practical activities that can help us in this process of re-imagining. Rooted in ancient philosophy – notably Socratic dialogue in Greece, which used questions to prompt self-discovery and growth – life, career, business and leadership coaching tools and techniques can help us shape a life we want to get out of bed for, step by step.

Perhaps you only want to make a few simple changes. Perhaps you'd like to dream big. To get out of a rut, a toxic relationship, or a job that isn't serving you. To plan a career change, start your own business, or retire. You might need to move house, get healthier or start afresh with everything. Whatever your desires, coaching can help you sort, sift, dream and devise, to create a more enticing existence.

Coaching can help you:

- Gain clarity on what truly matters.
- Find motivation and stay inspired.
- Stay accountable with regular check-ins.
- See fresh perspectives and uncover blind spots.
- Break big goals into manageable steps.
- Grow both personally and professionally.

Take time out to coach your own life

To help you start the process in your own space, for the last retreat in this book, I've created a five-day retreat on which you can coach your own life. Each day includes tips from coaching mentors, personal strategists and guides who have inspired me on my life journey at different hosted retreats.

This can be a full five-day retreat in your chosen retreat space for a fully immersive process, focusing on one core coaching subject a day for spaciousness. If you can't manage five days all in one go, you could treat each coaching subject as an individual, one-day retreat, and pepper those days throughout a longer period of time. Each retreat builds on the last, so they will work best if you complete them in the order laid out below.

Suggested schedule

Day one: Discover your core values

Day two: Work on your wheel of life

Day three: Reframe your limiting beliefs

Day four: Envision a new direction

Day five: Create and consolidate

Day one: Discover your core values

Our core values shape who we really are and how we live. Whether we recognise them or not, they serve as our guiding principles that influence our decisions, how we present ourselves and how our bodies respond to life. Knowing our values enables us to better navigate our life, career and relationships.

As holistic life and business coach Tara O'Rourke explains: 'When you feel truly alive in your life and work, you are living your values. Experiencing excitement and contentment, honouring something beyond just the tasks. Whereas when a value is compromised, you may sense it through a gut feeling or a tightness in your body, or act in ways that seem defensive or powerless.'

Taking time to understand your values can change everything, says Tara. 'You become more aware of why you've made a stand for something, chosen to speak up, or indeed to remain silent.' Examples of values include authenticity, equality, trustworthiness, professionalism, security, beauty, courage and so on. Anything goes. What will yours be? Follow the schedule below to find out, which I've devised in collaboration with Tara.

MORNING

Just Sit: On waking, take your journal or loose paper, and settle somewhere comfortable. Then sit quietly, with your hands on your heart, for a moment. Ask yourself the question, 'Who am I?' Take a moment, then write down everything that comes to mind. Peel away the layers of labels – such as teacher, lawyer, chef, parent – to go deeper. You might find yourself identifying as a kind person with strength, an advocate for those in need, someone who values equal education, a lover of animals and so on. Write a list of all the phrases that feel honest and right to you.

Reflect: Look at your phrases. How does each make you feel? What stands out as important? Distil these things into single words – 'I believe in access to education' could become 'equality' or 'fairness', for example, while 'I am someone who puts the best of me into my work' could become 'professionalism' or 'competency'.

Group: Next, look for common themes among your words. Group similar ones together and narrow them down to a single word. Truth and honesty could just become 'truth', 'equality' and 'fairness' could just become 'fairness', and so on.

Identify: Out of your list, identify your core values. Remember, if everything is a value, then nothing is, so limit your selection to five. Write down these values on a fresh piece of paper, or on a clean page in your journal.

Assess: Reflect on each value and ask yourself: 'Do I live by this value?' Living in alignment with your values brings a sense of aliveness and heartfelt knowing. For example, if your values include connection and trust, and your job involves having honest, inspiring conversations, you will feel true satisfaction and joy because you are living those values. For the values you currently do not embody, ask yourself how you behave, and how you feel, when they are compromised. If a compromised value is 'respect', where in your life do you feel disrespected, and how does that make you feel and behave?

AFTERNOON

Process: Take yourself for a walk to help you process what you have covered this morning. Let go of any 'trying'. On your return, write down anything that has occurred to you, to help you consolidate your morning activity. There will be times in life when you need to make changes to your job, lifestyle or relationships, if your values are consistently being compromised. Are there areas in your life where your values are being compromised, or where you know for sure they are not?

EVENING

Root: In your journal, draw a value tree. Start with the roots, and label them with your five core values. Then show how these roots connect into a trunk, branches, leaves and blossoms, right up to the blue sky of possibilities above. Use colours if you like and be as creative as you choose. The tree is you, and the roots are your foundational values – get to know them well.

Day two: Work on your wheel of life

A wheel of life is a fun and useful coaching tool that helps us to identify where we are 'at' in key areas of our lives. To see imbalance, neglected areas, where our values are consistently being compromised, or priorities for change.

Like a pie chart, a wheel of life is simply a circle, usually divided into eight segments, with each segment representing a core area of your life. These are personal to you, but could be things like: Friends and Family, Romance and Relationships, Health and Wellbeing, Personal and Spiritual Growth, Career and Work, Money and Finances, Fun and Free Time, and Community and Environment. Concentric circles inside the wheel, numbered 1 to 10, allow us to 'score' our satisfaction with each area.

Here's a simple example of a Wheel of Life:

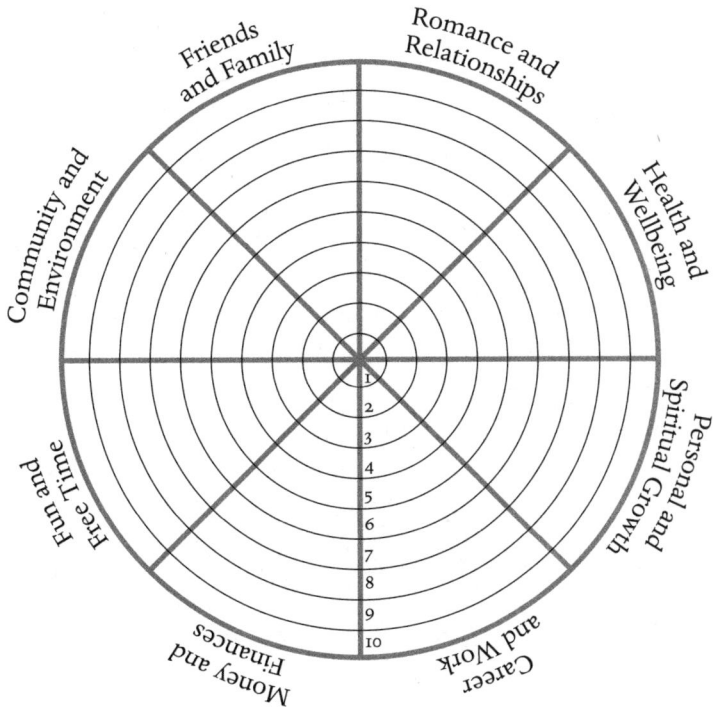

As mentor and coach Jessica McGregor Johnson explains: 'I've yet to meet anyone whose wheel segments aren't wonky!' Creating a wheel is an easy way to work out how to even things out in your life, if only a little. What shape will yours be? Follow the schedule below to find out, which I've devised in collaboration with Jessica.

MORNING

Reflect: On waking, re-read your list of values and look at your value tree from day one. Is there anything that particularly excites or interests you? Tap into that energy and bring it into your day.

Shape: To shape your wheel of life, start by deciding on the eight priority areas of your life, using the examples above to help you. Draw your wheel with eight segments and label them with words or phrases that resonate with you. Add your concentric circles, numbering the central circle 1, all the way out to 10. Rate your current satisfaction in each area of your life, with 10 being the highest score. When you have finished, draw a line in each segment that matches your score. If you want, colour the segments in. Someone's wonky wheel, for example, might look like the one opposite.

Consider: Next, take a moment to look at the shape of your wheel. Where are you out of balance? To help you go deeper and understand more, consider in your journal, or on loose paper, why you gave a particular area that score. Why exactly are your finances a three while your free time is a nine, for example? Add some honest detail to get a little clarity. Take a break whenever you need.

Explore: Start a fresh page in your journal or on loose paper and title it 'My Life'. List the core headings from your wheel of life beneath it, starting with the area that feels most out of balance to you. Write a paragraph for each, about what a 10 out of 10 might look and feel like in each area.

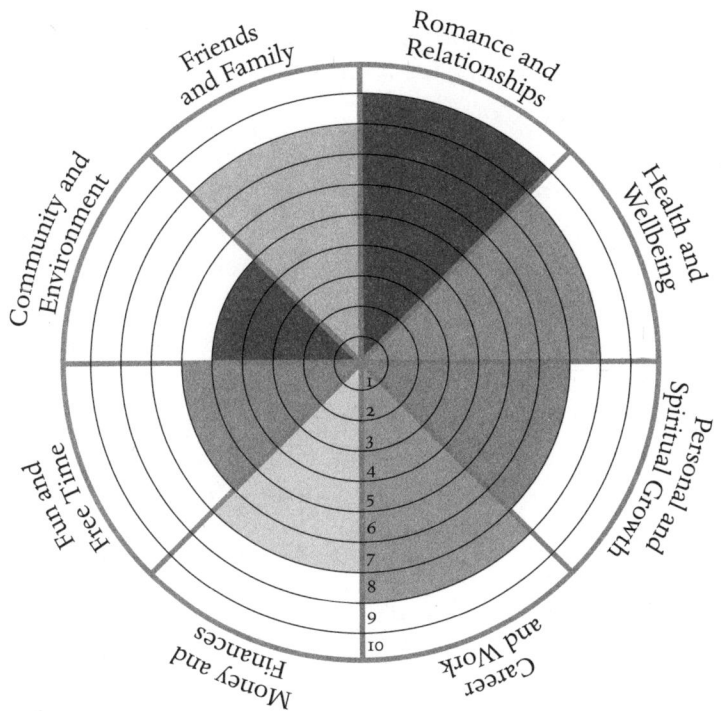

When you were scoring your wheel earlier, you subconsciously knew what a 10 out of 10 was to you. So don't censor yourself – the sky's the limit. When you have finished, jot down any quick headline ideas about how you might move your score closer to a 10 in each area.

AFTERNOON

Develop: After lunch, take yourself for an outing, ideally a walk in nature, to help you process what you have covered this morning and develop your ideas. Let go of any 'trying'. Take as much time as you need.

On your return, revisit your list of ideas and start to add more. Is there something else that's occurred to you on your walk? Think back to the values you created yesterday. Do you need to make some changes to help your scores increase in core areas, and live more in line with your values? What might those changes look like?

EVENING
Create: After your evening meal, settle yourself again somewhere warm and comfortable. Ask yourself, out of your ideas so far, which feels the most appealing and enticing for you? Translate it into colour using materials of your choice. Add colours in an abstract way to a blank page, or draw something simple that represents the idea. See what emerges. How might you turn this idea into reality? What's one thing you can do soon? Start to create an action plan for it.

If you feel energised to carry on, take yourself through your other ideas and jot down other tasks you could do that will help make them a reality. This is just the beginning of a process that can carry on over the following weeks and months, gradually moving your life into a better place for yourself.

Day three: Reframe your limiting beliefs

Do you believe something to be true about yourself that is holding you back in your life? All of us have what is known as 'limiting beliefs' – the thoughts, stories and patterns that stop us living the life we want and being who we want to be.

Career and personal coach Neeve Guinnane, who uses neuroscience in her work, explains: 'We all have things that we believe to be true, that are shaped from a very early age, by our environment, school, family, friends and experiences. These beliefs dictate how we show up in the world as adults, and how we see the world and ourselves. Some beliefs help us – for example, thinking you are lucky makes you notice more opportunities. But limiting beliefs hold us back from reaching our full potential.'

Does an area from the wheel of life you created on day two

need work because you have self-sabotaging beliefs about it? To identify and replace limiting beliefs with more empowering ones, follow the schedule below, which I've devised in collaboration with Neeve.

MORNING

Acknowledge: Take some time to look back at your list of values, your value tree, your wheel of life and the ideas and action plan you have started to create. Which area of your life feels the most 'stuck'? Pick one. Then sit comfortably, with feet on the ground, and take a few deep breaths to calm your nervous system.

In your journal or on loose paper, divide a page into two columns. Label the first column Limiting Belief and the second column Empowering Belief. In the first, write down the thoughts or beliefs that hold you back in your chosen area. Be curious, not judgemental. For example, a common belief might be: 'I am not good enough'.

Replace: In your Empowering Belief column, write down what you would like to believe instead about yourself in your chosen area of life. This doesn't have to be the opposite of the limiting belief, but rather something empowering. For example, if the limiting belief is 'I am not good enough', an empowering belief could be 'I am enough just as I am' or 'I do my best, and my best is good enough'.

Now, cancel the old belief. Literally strike through the limiting belief with your pen while saying aloud 'this is no longer true for me', or 'cancel this thought'. Verbally affirming this helps your brain recognise the shift.

To reinform this new empowering belief about the chosen area of your life that feels the most stuck, consistently repeat it throughout the day. This positive repetition builds stronger neural pathways, gradually transforming it into an ingrained belief.

AFTERNOON

Embody: Imagine how someone would behave if they held your empowering belief. How would they show up in the world? Write it down in your journal. For example, they might stand a little taller, look people in the eye, have an air of confidence and lead conversations with curiosity. You decide the behaviours you want to put into practice.

Then take yourself on an outing, ideally a walk in nature. Go slowly, and be present, engaging all your senses as you move. At the start of your walk, silently or aloud, repeat the empowering belief you created. Connect with the words as you walk. Ease into acting the part you have created for yourself – walking taller, perhaps, or looking someone in the eye as you pass. It might feel unnatural initially, but consistent practice will make it feel more authentic over time, and this walk is a good place to start. When you return, take a moment to thank yourself for your commitment to this positive change.

EVENING

Rehearse: Each time you reinforce your new belief and embody it, you strengthen the new neural pathways. Your brain will begin to scan for evidence that aligns with your new perspective, reinforcing your new mindset, and today is just the start. So to close the day, picture yourself already living your desired life, according to the empowering belief you created for yourself earlier. What emotions are you feeling as you visualise? Notice them, but then also practise feeling them, as if they are already true.

Day four: Envision a new direction

Today is about peeking into a preferable future by looking ahead five years. As Conscious Leadership Coach Julie Hosler explains: 'This is purely an imaginative exercise; it is not a feasibility study. "How" is not part of this conversation, so you can give your critical self the day off. If you are surfing in the morning and skiing in the evening, that is fine. The less sense it makes, the better it gets.' To see how this might work, follow the schedule below, which I've devised in collaboration with Julie.

MORNING

Pick: Open your journal and look back over your values, your wheel of life, your ideas and action lists, and the new empowering belief you came up with on day three. Ask yourself, is there an obvious part of your life that you would like to seriously change? Or something you want to bring forwards into your preferable future? It could be something relatively small, such as a daily routine, or something much bigger, like a change to your career, home or a significant relationship. Pick one and write it in your journal, or on loose paper, under the heading 'A New Direction'.

Dream: Settle yourself, return to your journal and give yourself uninterrupted time to write freely about your ideal future. Project your life five years from now. How old will you be? Imagine that you are in an ideal situation in your chosen area, and that everything that you tried for, you have succeeded at. To help activate your imagination, you could play creatively stimulating, instrumental music that appeals to you.

As Julie says: 'Dream big. Really go there in your mind as if it is already happening. Don't hold back, and don't edit. Describe a specific day in this imagined future. Go into as much detail as you'd like. Write in full sentences and paragraphs. Keep writing until you have nothing else to write. Do not direct your imagination – just allow things to come in.'

Here are prompts to get your creative juices flowing:

- ✧ Where are you living (city/country, flat/house)?
- ✧ How and what time do you start your day?
- ✧ What type of work are you doing?

- How are you looking after your wellbeing?
- What are you eating?
- What are you reading/wearing/making/creating/learning?
- Who are you spending time and sharing space with?
- What are you talking about with people?
- What questions are you exploring?
- What is the next big thing on the horizon for you?

AFTERNOON

Process: After lunch, get outside for a walk, ideally in nature. A few times, while you are moving, repeat an affirmation inside your mind or aloud that relates to the work you have just done, such as, 'I am open and willing to receive this preferable future'. See Affirm, p. 143, for more on this.

EVENING

Plan: After your evening meal, start to integrate your vision and plan purposeful steps forwards by writing in your journal or on loose paper:

- Three people you know who can support your future vision
- What resources you currently have to make this preferable future possible
- Three qualities or skills you'll need most in order to achieve this future
- What you need to eliminate to allow space for this vision to grow
- What you need to remind yourself as you move in this direction

- ✧ What simple steps you can take in the next thirty days to take things forward

Day five: Create and consolidate

Over the last four days you have covered a lot. Give yourself a final day to relax, reflect and consolidate what you have processed so far.

MORNING

Let your morning unfold as you see fit, ideally giving yourself a long lie-in to start. You could do all or just one of the following exercises:

- ✧ Revisit your values from day one and check they feel right to you.

- ✧ Revisit your wheel of life from day two and add to the list of ideas and tasks you started that will help you move towards a score of '10' in important areas.

- ✧ Look at your limiting belief from day three. Practise embodying your new empowering belief, by feeling and behaving accordingly. Or are there other limiting beliefs you could acknowledge and replace using the same process today?

- ✧ Look at the three people you named who might support your future vision. Jot down what specific ways they could support you. Consider setting a time to meet them for a chat in the coming weeks. Ask yourself, is there anyone else you trust you can enlist to support you?

- ✧ Look at the rest of the notes you made at the end of day four to help you take purposeful steps forwards in your desired new direction. Anything to change, add or refine?

When you have had enough, end your morning with movement in the fresh air and some lunch.

AFTERNOON

Have fun consolidating your new ideas and plans, by creating either a vision notebook or a vision board, or both. These will serve as a reminder and motivator after your retreat as you move towards your new goals.

Vision notebook: Start a fresh notebook with a list of your values from day one, and if you like, a copy of your values tree, coloured in as you see fit. Then write out clean lists of what is important to you from the last four days. This could be the core areas of your life where you desire change, the ideas and plans you have to help make them happen, any new empowering beliefs you have devised for yourself, and the purposeful steps you're planning to move you in a new direction.

Vision board: Choose the dream that is most important and compelling to you, and create a vision board for it. This is a collage of images, words and symbols that represent the future you're stepping into. Let yourself be creative. This is a fun activity to do with someone else, especially a friend, older child or teenager who might also want to create a vision board for themselves (see Retreating with others, p. 20).

Take time to flick through and cut out words, pictures and photos from newspapers, magazines and other materials you may have about the chosen dream aspect of your life. Arrange and stick them on an A3 piece of card or corkboard as you see fit, in as packed or as spacious a way as you choose. Write or paint phrases or words around them that relate to your dream. Keep adding and refining until you are happy with your creation.

If you're creating a vision board about working from home, for example, because you currently work in an office and want a change, you might choose: pictures or photographs of a colourful or peaceful home workspace, something that represents a flexible daily schedule, outdoor activities you'd like to do from your door, from nature walks to wild water dips, and other symbols that say 'freedom' or 'focus' to you. You could add empowering words such as 'ease' or 'my time, my terms', and images that capture the energy of your ideal workday, whether that's short, calm, productive or self-directed. Feel free – anything goes.

EVENING

Put your vision book and/or board somewhere easy to see and access, so you can revisit them regularly over the coming days and weeks. At some point, perhaps after your evening meal, try Julie Hosler's Copper Coil Exercise below. This fun and effective ten-minute daydream gives your mind an opportunity to wander in the direction of your vision, and help change the neuropathways in your brain. Repeat it wherever and whenever you need.

Copper coil exercise: Settle yourself somewhere comfortable and set a timer for ten minutes. Imagine coiling a thick copper wire around your body. Begin winding it around you at your base, around your mid-section, torso, neck and head. Imagine one end is connected to the ground underneath you; the other end extends from the top of your head into the space above you and continues from there into the outermost space that you can no longer see.

As the coil binds to you, close your eyes. Imagine what it feels like to have accomplished your vision for your next chapter in life. If you cannot imagine the specifics, imagine how you will feel, what your days would entail, where you are, who is there, and what are you likely to overhear or to be heard saying. Continue this until the timer gives you a nudge.

Now imagine that the copper wire is acting as a magnetic property to the thoughts and visions that you have just explored. They are all drawn to the copper wire and magnetised to it, because it is coiled around you. Release the wire and its magnetic effect, and say aloud: 'This or something better is happening for my highest good and the highest good of others. Thank you.'

Tips for a successful practice

- Know that change takes time, so whatever direction your coaching retreat days take you in, be patient and kind to yourself. Leave lots of spaciousness inside and around each day, to give your unconscious time to work.

- If things are becoming too intense, simply stop and do something different – work out, have a bath, or share a meal with a friend to chat things over. Each afternoon, it's important to put down your tools and get outside.

Reflect on your practice

For a few evenings following your retreat, take time to check into your thoughts and feelings, and note any new revelations that have presented themselves. Refer back to your vision notebook and/or board. Allow your ideas and plans to percolate.

Continue your practice

Your self-devised coaching retreat is just the start of change. Continue visualising your ideal goals and beliefs, and the feelings they create, and behave as if you are already embodying them to help make them possible. Neuroscience shows that the brain uses very similar processes for both reality and visualisation, as coach Neeve Guinnane explains: 'When you practise visualisation, your brain treats it almost like a real experience, which can help turn your dreams into reality.' It might feel uncomfortable or awkward, but the secret is to just do it anyway. It will feel more authentic over time.

Finding a guide: You can revisit the coaching activities you have experienced at any time in your life, choosing those that have worked particularly well for you. To go into detail on a particular issue or for more guidance and motivation, you might like the support of a coach, mentor or strategist. Who you choose is important, for much like choosing a counsellor or a Yoga teacher, how you relate to them will be key to your progress. Always have a no-obligations call first. For suggestions, see Resources, p. 261.

Hosted coaching retreats

Some holistic retreats offer one-off and fun interactive group coaching workshops to help you tackle small things in life that can make a big difference, such as how to plan your day, make confident decisions or set healthy boundaries. They often include vision boarding in a group, which can be fun and motivating. Other retreats have life, career or leadership coaches you can book private sessions with, to help you tackle something specific, with follow-ups for when you return home.

Dedicated coaching retreats offer more immersive experiences, to help you at different life stages, whether you are looking for life and relationship coaching, business, career and leadership coaching, or retirement planning. They mix one-to-one sessions with group workshops, and include lots of downtime to rest and digest your process in remarkable locations. Private coaching retreats are more intense experiences, where you will have the devoted attention of one coach and be able to fast-track any changes you need.

REFERENCES

Introduction

Mary Oliver, 'The Summer Day' (Reprinted by the permission of The Charlotte Sheedy Literary Agency as agent for the author. Copyright © 1990, 2006, 2008, 2017 by Mary Oliver with permission of Bill Reichblum).

Your Retreat Toolkit

Vita Sackville-West, *In Your Garden* (Michael Joseph, 1951: Reproduced with permission of Curtis Brown Group Ltd, London, on behalf of The Beneficiaries of the Estate of Vita Sackville West. Copyright © Vita Sackville West).

Søren Kierkegaard, letter to his niece, Henriette Lund, in 1847, from *A Short Life of Kierkegaard* (Oxford University Press, 1938, translated by Walter Lowrie).

Virginia Woolf, *A Room of One's Own* (Hogarth Press, 1929).

Rebecca Andrist, founder of Jiva Healing (https://jivahealing.com). For more information, see Jan Chozen Bays, *Mindful Eating: A Guide to Rediscovering a Healthy and Joyful Relationship with Food* (Shambhala Publications, 2017 revised edition).

Purge

Theresa Lola, 'To My Previous Self', *Ceremony for the Nameless* (Penguin Press, 2024). p. 76.

Julia Cameron, *The Artist's Way* (Pan Books, 1992).

For more on wild swimming, see Dr Mark Harper, 'The Science of Cold Water Swimming', Outdoor Swimming Society, https://www.outdoorswimmingsociety.com.

Francine Jay, *The Joy of Less: A Minimalist Guide to Declutter, Organize, and Simplify* (Chronicle Books, 2016).

Marie Kondo, *The Life-Changing Magic of Tidying: A simple, effective way to banish clutter forever* (Vermilion, 2014).

For more information, see Tiffanie Darke, *What to Wear and Why: Your Guilt-Free Guide to Sustainable Fashion* (Broadleaf Books, 2024).

Connect

Danusha Laméris, 'Small Kindnesses', *Bonfire Opera* (University of Pittsburgh Press, 2020: Reprinted with kind permission from Danusha Laméris).

Sylvia Plath, *The Bell Jar* (Heinemann, 1963).

Malala Yousafzai, *I Am Malala: How One Girl Stood Up for Education and Changed the World* (Orion Children's Books, 2014).

William Wordsworth, from a letter to his wife, Mary, dated 29 April 1812, *The Love Letters of William and Mary Wordsworth*, ed. Beth Darlington (Cornell University Press, 2009).

Emma Clark (https://emma-clark.com) and Satish Kumar (https://www.satishkumarfoundation.co.uk) in conversation at a 'Gardening as a spiritual practice' retreat at the Dartington Estate, Devon, England (https://www.dartington.org).

Elizabeth Von Armin, *The Solitary Summer* (Macmillan, 1929).

Ella Wheeler Wilcox, 'The World's Need', *Complete Poetical Works of Ella Wheeler Wilcox* (Delphi Classics, 2016).

Kio Stark, *When Strangers Meet: How People You Don't Know Can Transform You* (Simon & Schuster, 2016).

Anne Herbert, 'Random Kindness and Senseless Acts of Beauty', *Whole Earth Review*, July 1985.

Ramiro Ortega (https://www.ramiroortega.com) spoke at a mindfulness retreat at Sharpham House, Devon, England (https://www.sharphamtrust.org).

For more on befriending, see Christina Feldman, *Boundless Heart: The Buddha's Path of Kindness, Compassion, Joy, and Equanimity* (Shambhala Publications Inc, 2017).

Emily Dickinson, 'They might not need me', *Emily Dickinson's Poems: As She Preserved Them* (Harvard University Press, 2016), p. 717.

Create

Anatole France, *The Garden of Epicurus* (First published 1908; English translation published by Bodley Head, 1923).

Adrian Hill, *Art Versus Illness: A Story of Art Therapy* (George Allen & Unwin, 1945).

Penelope Orfanoudaki, art therapist and founder of Artful Retreats (https://www.artfulretreats.com).

Georgia O'Keeffe, foreword of the catalogue for the show at the Anderson Galleries in New York, 1926, reproduced with kind permission of the Georgia O'Keeffe Museum.

Mihaly Csikszentmihalyi, *Flow: The Psychology of Optimal Experience* (Harper Perennial, 2008).

From a lecture given at Leighton Park School by Vanessa Bell, reproduced in Vanessa Bell, *Sketches in Pen and Ink: A Bloomsbury Notebook*, ed. Lia Giachero (The Hogarth Press, 1997: Reproduced with kind permission from the Estate of Vanessa Bell).

Josh Dickson, trauma therapist and founder of Resurface surf-therapy retreats (https://resurfaceuk.com).

For more on the vagus nerve, see Jessica Maguire, *The Nervous System Reset: Overcome Pain, Trauma and Stress Using Your Vagus Nerve* (Pan Macmillan, 2024).

Kelly Lambert, *Lifting Depression: A Neuroscientist's Hands-on Approach to Activating Your Brain's Healing Power* (Basic Books, 2008: Reprinted by permission of Basic Books, an imprint of Hachette Book Group, Inc).

Erin Dale (https://www.erindalemovement.com) is part of The Nest retreat in Cornwall, England (https://thenestlife.co.uk).

Amy Lowell, *Twenty-Four Hokku on a Modern Theme* (1921).

Nurture

Dean Atta, 'On Days When', *There is (still) love here* (Nine Arches Press, 2022: Published by permission of Nine Arches Press www.ninearchespress.com).

For more on Glenn Ceresoli, see https://yogamind.com.au.

Giles Andreae, *Giraffes Can't Dance*, illustrated by Guy Parker-Rees (Orchard Books, 1999).

Beverley Nichols, *Down the Garden Path* (1932).

For more on the 'Fuck It Life' movement, see https://thefuckitlife.com.

Frances Hodgson Burnett, *The Making of a Marchioness* (Persephone Books, 2001).

For more on sleep, see Dr Nerina Ramlakhan, *Tired but Wired: How to Overcome Your Sleep Problems – The Essential Sleep Toolkit* (Souvenir Press, 2010).

Rainer Maria Rilke, *Letters on Life: New Prose Translations*, translated by Ulrich Baer (Penguin Classics, 2007).

Trust

Henry David Thoreau, from the 'Economy' chapter in *Walden* (Macmillan Collector's Library, 2004).

Émile Coué, *Self-Mastery Through Conscious Autosuggestion* (1922).
L. M. Montgomery, *Anne of Green Gables* (1908).
Ralph Waldo Emerson, *Self-Reliance* (Thames and Hudson, 2021).
Helen Hull, *Heat Lightning* (Persephone Books, 2013: Reprinted with kind permission of Persephone Books).

Reclaim

Adelaide Love, from a poem in *The Slender Singing Tree* (Dodd, Mead and Company, 1933).
Jillian Lavender spoke at a London Meditation Centre Rounding Retreat (londonmeditationcentre.com) held at Broughton Sanctuary in Yorkshire, England (https://broughtonsanctuary.co.uk). Also see Jillian Lavender, *Why Meditate? Because it works* (Yellow Kite, 2021) and https://jillianlavender.com.
Kate Emmerson, coach and retreat facilitator (https://www.kate-emmerson.com).
Fiona Arrigo, founder of The Arrigo programme (https://thearrigoprogramme.com).
Dr Anna Lembke, *Dopamine Nation: Finding Balance in the Age of Indulgence* (Headline, 2021).

Settle

John O'Donohue, excerpt from the blessing 'For One Who is Exhausted', *Benedictus: A Book of Blessings* (Bantam Press, 2007: Reprinted with kind permission of the John O'Donohue Legacy Partnership).
For more on the breath, see James Nestor, *Breath: The New Science of a Lost Art* (Riverhead Books, 2020) and Dan Brule, *Just Breathe: Mastering Breathwork* (Enliven Books, 2018).
Eckhart Tolle, *The Power of Now: A Guide to Spiritual Enlightenment* (Hodder & Stoughton, 2001).
Billy Collins, 'The Present', *The Rain in Portugal: Poems* (Random House, 2016). Used by permission of Random House, an

imprint and division of Penguin Random House LLC. All rights reserved).

Jon Kabat-Zinn, *Wherever You Go, There You Are: Mindfulness meditation for everyday life* (Balance, 1993. Reprinted by permission of Balance, an imprint of Hachette Book Group, Inc).

Erling Kagge, *Silence: In the Age of Noise* (Viking, 2017).

For more on Gaia House in Devon, England, see https://gaiahouse.co.uk.

Plan

Cleo Wade, 'that sounds great' (Reproduced with kind permission of Cleo Wade, https://cleowade.com).

Cognitive Load Theory (CLT) was formulated by John Sweller, in his foundational 1988 paper 'Cognitive Load During Problem Solving: Effects on Learning'.

See Barry Schwartz, *The Paradox of Choice: Why More is Less* (HarperCollins, 2024).

See Roy Baumeister, *Willpower: Rediscovering the Greatest Human Strength* (Penguin Press, 2011).

'Planning fallacy' was a term coined by psychologists Daniel Kahneman and Amos Tversk, see Daniel Kahneman, *Thinking, Fast and Slow* (Farrar, Straus & Giroux, 2011).

See Cal Newport, *Deep Work: Rules for Focused Success in a Distracted World* (Grand Central Publishing, 2016).

The Zeigarnik Effect, after Bluma Zeigarnik's 1927 research paper 'On Finished and Unfinished Tasks'.

Henry David Thoreau, *Walden* (Macmillan Collector's Library, 2004).

The 10/10/10 rule was a clever method devised by Chip and Dan Heath in their book *Decisive* (Crown Currency, 2013).

For more on Tania Carrière, see https://www.advivumjourneys.ca.

For more on Tara O'Rourke, see https://www.saolbeo.ie.

For more on Jessica McGregor Johnson, see https://jessicamcgregorjohnson.com.

For more on Neeve Guinnane, see https://becoachingsolutions.com.

For more on Julie Hosler, see http://www.thestrategicspace.com.

Retreat Poems

A version of 'Small Group Gathering' was first published by Carcanet Press in *PN Review*, Issue 271, May/June 2023 (https://www.pnreview.co.uk).

'Silent Retreat at Gaia House' was first published as 'At Gaia House in Devon' by Carcanet Press in *PN Review*, Issue 271, May/June 2023 (https://www.pnreview.co.uk).

RESOURCES

Introduction

Mind-body connection: For more on neuroscience and the mind-body connection, see Candace Pert, *Molecules of Emotion: Why You Feel the Way You Feel* (Prentice, Hall & IBD, 1997). For more on neuroplasticity, see Norman Doidge, *The Brain That Changes Itself: Stories of Personal Triumph from the Frontiers of Brain Science* (Viking, 2007).

Retreat Recipes: For delicious, cleansing and gut-friendly recipes on your self-devised retreats, I recommend those in books by nutritional therapist Amanda Hamilton, who has free recipes at www.amandahamilton.com/blogs/recipes and runs retreats and coaching programmes, and by nutritional therapist Jeanette Hyde, especially *The Gut Makeover* (Quercus, 2016), and who has recipes and food tips at The Gut Makeover Substack (https://thegutmakeover.substack.com/).

Purge

Ayurvedic practitioners: For reliable Ayurvedic practitioners in the UK, I recommend Andy Shakeshaft of Essential Ayurveda (https://www.essentialayurveda.co.uk/pages/ayurvedic-consultations). For more information, see the Ayurvedic Professionals Association in the UK (https://apa.uk.com) or the Association of Ayurvedic Professionals of North America in the US (https://www.aapna.org).

Connect

Gardening: For general gardening advice, I recommend Monty Don (www.montydon.com), the Royal Horticultural Society (rhs.org.uk) in the UK, and the American Horticultural Society (ahsgardening.org) in the US. The UK charity Thrive has easy-to-follow resources for therapeutic and creative gardening (thrive.org.uk).

Create

Art therapists: For qualified art therapists see the directories organised by the British Association of Art Therapists (baat.org) and the American Art Therapy Association (arttherapy.org). I also recommend workshops and retreats with Penelope Orfanoudaki of Artful Retreats (artfulretreats.com).

Creativity as bravery: For more on the courage you need for art, see the inspirational *Big Magic: Creative living beyond fear* (Bloomsbury Publishing, 2015) by Elizabeth Gilbert.

Online creativity clubs: In the UK, The Royal Academy in London often runs online Sketch Clubs (https://www.royalacademy.org.uk/page/saturday-sketch-club), whilst The Arvon Foundation offers oodles of online writing workshops and retreats (https://www.arvon.org/arvon-at-home/).

Nurture

Ecstatic Dance facilitators: Ecstatic Dance Global (ecstaticdance.org) is an international non-profit directory of dance facilitators and events.

Pilates teachers: The Pilates Foundation (pilatesfoundation.com) has a UK directory of certified Pilates instructors. In the US, see the Pilates Method Alliance (pilatesmethodalliance.org).

Qigong teachers: Try the self-paced courses devised by Mimi Kuo Deemer (mkdeemer.com), while Chinese Medicine Practitioner Katie Brindle has lots of free resources (katiebrindle.com). The Tai Chi Union for Great Britain (taichiunion.com) lists registered Qigong instructors in the UK. In the US, see the National Qigong Association (https://www.nqa.org).

Tai Chi teachers: The Tai Chi Union for Great Britain (taichiunion.com) lists registered tai chi instructors in the UK. In the US, see The Tai Chi Foundation (taichifoundation.org).

Somatic movement practitioners: The International Somatic Movement Education and Therapy Association (ISMETA) has a global directory of qualified practitioners (https://ismeta.org).

Yoga teachers: For online classes, try a membership-based platform such as https://movementformodernlife.com. The British Wheel of Yoga (bwy.org.uk) in the UK has an directory of accredited Yoga teachers. In the US, see Yoga Alliance (yogaalliance.org).

Bathing: For enticing ways to make the most out of bathing experiences of all kinds, see *Bathe: Rediscover the Ancient Art of Relaxation* (Lagom, 2018) by Suzanne Duckett.

Therapy: For psychotherapy and other therapies, as well as useful resources for living well, a reliable starting point is The School of Life (https://www.theschooloflife.com/online-psychotherapy/). The British Association for Counselling and Psychotherapy (BACP) Therapist Directory (bacp.co.uk) lists qualified UK therapists; in the US, see Psychology Today's directory (psychologytoday.com).

Vedic Meditation teachers: I recommend Jillian Lavender and Michael Miller, co-founders of the London and New York Meditation Centres, who teach beginners and advanced techniques in London and New York, run retreats in the UK, India and Europe, and offer regular online sessions followed by talks on life (londonmeditationcentre.com; newyorkmeditationcenter.com). Other reliable teachers around the world can be found at learnvedicmeditation.co. Research and talk to any teacher before committing, to check you feel a resonance with them.

Settle

Breathwork teachers: There are lots of breathwork teachers across the globe who offer private sessions, courses and retreats in person and online. Research them thoroughly, and talk to them on a call before committing, to check you feel a resonance with them. For online and in-person sessions, workshops and retreats, I recommend Rebecca Dennis (breathingtree.co.uk) and Justine Clement in the UK (wonderbreath.co). Other reliable teachers include founder of Breathguru® Alan Dolan in the UK and Lanzarote and his graduates (https://www.breathguru.com/); and somatic coach Ian Stratton in the US (https://ianstratton.me).

For more on mindfulness: Dr Jon Kabat-Zinn, the founder of mindfulness-based stress reduction (MBSR), makes mindfulness accessible to everyone. He has lots of free online resources, and runs online and in-person mindfulness retreats (jonkabat-zinn.com). I also recommend anything by the late Vietnamese Zen master and peace activist Thich Nhat Hanh, especially *Peace Is Every Step: The Path of Mindfulness in Everyday Life* (Rider, 1995), which shows how mindfulness can turn life's regular pressures into sources of understanding and opportunities for change.

For more on Buddhism: *Buddhism Without Beliefs: A Contemporary Guide to Awakening* (Bloomsbury Publishing, 1998) by Stephen Batchelor is an accessible introduction to the philosophy. I also recommend *The Art of Happiness* (Riverhead Books, 1998) by the Dalai Lama, books and talks by Insight Meditation teacher and co-founder of Gaia House and Bodhi College Christina Feldman (https://dharmaseed.org/teacher/44/), and podcasts, videos and books by American Buddhist nun Pema Chödrön (https://pemachodronfoundation.org).

Plan

Coaches, mentors and strategists: For online and in-person private sessions, workshops and retreats I recommend: Julie Hosler (thestrategicspace.com) in France and the US; Rosie Walford (thebigstretch.com) in New Zealand; Tania Carrière (advivumjourneys.ca) in Canada, Mexico and Europe; Kate Emmerson (kate-emmerson.com) in Scotland and Europe; Tara O'Rourke (saolbeo.ie) and Neeve Guinnane (becoachingsolutions.com) in Ireland; Jessica McGregor Johnson (jessicamcgregorjohnson.com) in Spain. For directories of other accredited life and career coaches, see the Association for Coaching (associationforcoaching.com) in the UK and the International Coaching Federation (coachingfederation.org) in the US.

BOOKS TO RETREAT WITH

My small and personal selection of suggestions include:

For creative inspiration: *Colours of Art: The Story of Art in 80 Palettes* (Frances Lincoln, 2022), by art critic Chloë Ashby, features an astonishing array of paintings and their glorious colour palettes throughout history, with engaging write-ups about each one of them.

For delight: *The Book of Delights* (Hodder & Stoughton, 2020), by poet Ross Gay, features heart-boosting essayettes that find the joy in miniscule everyday experiences, from getting lost and writing by hand to the pecan nut.

For dealing with daily life: *Wherever You Go, There You Are: Mindfulness meditation for everyday life* (Piatkus, 2004), by mindfulness pioneer Jon Kabat-Zinn, is a clever and humane look at how mindfulness helps us meet life wisely as it comes. It's easy to dip in and out of. Parents in particular might relish his section 'Parenting as a practice'.

For dealing with difficulty: *When Things Fall Apart: Heart Advice for Difficult Times* (Shambhala Publications, 2002), by American Buddhist nun Pema Chödrön, offers a consoling Buddhist perspective on how to meet life's challenges and face discomfort with openness instead of turning away.

For being alone: *Solitude* (HarperCollins Publishers 1997), by psychiatrist and psychoanalyst Anthony Storr, intelligently explores the creative and intellectual benefits of spending time away from others, and challenges the belief that happiness depends only on close relationships.

For understanding silence: *Silence in the Age of Noise* (Viking, 2017), by Norwegian explorer Erling Kagge, draws on his experience of a solo fifty-day trek across Antarctica to contemplate how enriching silence can be. I also love *A Time To Keep Silence* (John Murray, 2004), by travel writer Patrick Leight

Fermor, a portrayal of various monasteries and his occasional retreats in them.

For women: *Gift From The Sea* (Vintage Books, 1991), by Anne Morrow Lindbergh, was written in the 1950s during a brief retreat on Captiva Island in Florida, but still feels relevant to us today. It's a lyrical meditation on womanhood and the search for simplicity, graced by delicate drawings of shells.

For poetry: I love the accessible mix of brilliant poems in anthologies such as the Poetry Prescription series (Macmillan) and The Poetry Pharmacy series (Penguin).

For more information, see A Pause For Reading on p. 29.

HOSTED RETREATS

In each chapter of this book I explain the types of hosted, residential retreats available around the world related to particular themes. They come in many forms, from private, bespoke retreats you can arrange to suit you, to holistic havens and health retreats that are open all year round, and group adventures that run on set dates.

You can go on a hosted retreat to change your life, work through emotional issues, ease your grief, sadness, anxiety or depression, get fitter, learn something new, reconnect with nature, be creative in all sorts of ways, sort out a medical health issue, be in solitude, relate to like-minded others, or simply relax, away from the hustle and bustle of the world.

On the best of them, you are nurtured and cooked for, fully supported in whatever process you are going through, and have the time and space to rest in a beautiful location specially designed for retreating.

As with the self-devised retreats in this book, the success of hosted retreats lies in how much of yourself you bring to them. Be honest with yourself, before you book, about what it is you really need. Often, it's the thing we feel most fearful of that has the potential to transform us the most.

Go alone if you need real space, to work things through, or be free of your back story. There's a subtle, heart-warming camaraderie that can develop between people on a cleverly curated retreat, most especially when you are amongst 'new' people – many of whom may then turn into friends. Alternatively, enjoy time out replenishing and reconnecting with those you love.

The choice of hosted retreats around the world is now vast and bewildering. Select with care. You can find many of the most iconic, reliable retreats I have experienced on Queen of Retreats, a carefully curated retreat platform which I founded in 2011. Trust is at the heart of what we do. We feature stories about people's real-life experiences of retreats, and unlike listings sites, we turn away retreats that are not the real deal. You'll find us at www.queenofretreats.com.

RETREAT POEMS

Here are five of my poems that have emerged from retreating experiences, and that I have referenced throughout this book. See A word about poetry, p. 9, for more information.

Small Group Gathering

I did not go.
I waited till late
to decide yes or no.

The rain may have played a part.
It was hard, too wet to wear
my new sheer skirt.

I'd been prepared to drive, to say:
just a cup of tea please.
But who wants to arrive
in trousers you've worn before,

to sit tired and listen
in another person's kitchen,
while others share their thoughts,

and you try to work out
if you can share yours?

That night, I did not go.

See Say no, p. 169.

Acupuncture

One by one he pushed the small blunt points
into the skin across my shoulder, neck and head.

With each steel pinprick came tears for the week,
released into the towel around my face—

then more, till there was a pour,
with all my subtle griefs inside it—

our midnight concerns, my second-guessing
the tone of a message, drizzle—till time was up,

needles gone, sopping cloth removed,
my upper body filled with microscopic holes—

do all your patients do this—often, yes—
outside with sunglassed eyes I find my car,

drive home to cry more in the garden,
till love erupts—

for you with your guitar in our kitchen,
for the song she is singing in her bedroom,

for the bulbs we planted last October,
turned into shoots on this February day,

pushing up out of the fresh bark,
threatening to pierce us with their beauty.

See Treat yourself, p. 126.

I am on a Zoom call
with my camera off,
stretching in front of my desk,
my arms above my head,
my toes away from my legs.

I hear a point of interest
but decide against contributing—
place my feet on the sheepskin,
circle my pupils inside closed lids
like a yogi taught us at that spa.

After listening I return to my chair,
put my hands through my hair,
smile, switch the camera on.
The sea of faces falters
for one moment, carries on.

I check the clock—
our time is nearly done,
but in my mind I leave
to put my trainers on,
head out into the air

across the fields of violet light,
with coconut gorse and terns in flight,
till I watch my fellow zoomers
exit one by one,
and I too can be gone.

See Unplug, p. 177.

How To Give What You Don't Need To The Sea

Go alone to Yarmer beach when it's deserted.
Remove your shoes, even in winter,
and walk barefoot through the crush of sand
to the clamorous shore. Close your eyes,
breathe in the brine and the roar.

Pitch your anxiety into the black,
name the person you think gave it to you,
the event—far past or yesterday—
you think made it for you.
Pitch it again louder. Give it some spit.

Undress, get in. Swim in the arresting cold
across the bay. Allow more anguish to fall in.
After five wide strokes, dive inside
the sweet salt deep. Keep moving
till your shocked body is full of heat.

Climb out, wait in this engulfed state.
Delight in the feel of the outdoor air
as it meets your charged skin.
Open your eyes, your bare arms wide
to the undyed sky and the granite rocks,

open your heart to the life that you are in.
Sift your patch for the smoothest pebble,
make it a memento you can clutch.
Get dressed, find your shoes,
resume living, rekindled from within.

See Refresh yourself, p. 51.

Silent Retreat at Gaia House

I met my fear in the heavy sky
that hid the blue we knew was there,
and under the staggering oak tree
where I felt only this high,

in the owl's call on the first night,
on the bed that was not mine,
and taking toast to the lounge
with the pots of red geraniums.

I met my fear, and then I lost her,
walking through the vegetable gardens,
lifting my feet up and placing them down,
circling the cemetery of nuns.

I somehow, somewhere, lost my fear,
and then I lost this.
I lost this, slowly,
then overnight, I lost that.

I lost this, then that,
then him, and all of them.
I was walking slowly
on wet evening grass,

barefoot alongside others
and I lost everything.
And drawing on the jacket of the breath,
I realised I was happy.

See Go into silence, p. 208.

ACKNOWLEDGEMENTS

I'd like to express my gratitude to everyone who has helped support me, both directly and indirectly, in the process of writing this book.

To all the exceptional retreat owners, leaders, mentors, coaches, teachers, therapists, writers, artists and thinkers who have helped shape this book, and who have helped shape me.

To the Creative Artists Agency, especially my vibrant UK agent Harriet Poland for her persistence, belief and support, Daisy Shayegan for her kind help handling permissions, Agnès Rigou for deftly handling rights, and Cindy Uh for championing the book in the US.

To the talented teams at my UK publisher Ebury and my US publisher Rodale, especially my Ebury editor Céline Elkouby Nyssens, for helping to shape the book so cleverly and with such kindness and patience. Also huge thanks to Rodale editor Donna Loffredo for her belief in the book from the get-go, Anya Hayes for her encouragement, copyeditor Anna Hervé for her clear thinking, Holly Ovenden for her enticing illustrations, Jonathan Baker for his lovely design, Kaitlin Beranek for the book's delicious finish, and Aisling O'Toole, Jasleen Dhindsa and Shasmin Mozomil for helping to spread the word.

To Michael Schmidt at Carcanet Press for his exciting belief in my work, and Professor Steve Ellis at the University of Birmingham for his empowering encouragement early on. To my fellow poets Kit Griffiths, Mike Farren and Mel Tibbs for their generous feedback, my colleague Christine Fieldhouse for her first reading, kindness and sense of fun, and my friend Jools Sampson of Reclaim Yourself for her grounding advice and hot tub camaraderie.

A special thanks from my nervous system to my remarkable Vedic Meditation teachers Jillian Lavender and Michael Miller, for teaching me a technique that resets it daily, and from my shoulders to my local massage therapist Sophia Loxton, for easing out their tension regularly.

To the dedicatees of this book, for gifting me the time and space to write it – my graceful business partner Victoria Spicer, and my precious pocket family Tom and Annoushka Sylge Jones. To my effervescent parents Ann and Herbie Sylge for their sustaining love and Sunday roasts, my brothers Chris and Olly Sylge for their sustaining sense of humour and remarkable families, and my childhood friend Fiona Vettiankal for all the love, laughter and nurturing mini-breaks.

To all my beautiful friends in Devon and beyond, for the touches of each of you in here, and for helping to make life delightful, most especially Caroline Dorich, Elle and Nick Franklin, Sophie Carr, Naomi Nightingale, Vanessa Worrall, Elly Reid, Sarah and Jeff Collinson, Clare and Jay Spanton, and in loving memory of Melanie Cutcliffe, now safely on the retreat for which we are all destined.

BIOGRAPHY

Caroline Sylge is a poet, author and journalist, and the founder of Queen of Retreats and The Global Retreat Company. She lives in Devon, England, with her husband and daughter.